DOGWISE

By the same author
WHY DOES MY DOG. . . ?

DOGWISE

The Natural Way to Train Your Dog

John Fisher

photographs by Tony Glue

SOUVENIR PRESS

First published 1992 by Souvenir Press Ltd,
43 Great Russell Street, London WC1B 3PA
and simultaneously in Canada

Reprinted 1994, 1996 (twice)

ISBN 0 285 63114 4

Printed in Great Britain by
St Edmundsbury Press Ltd, Bury St Edmunds, Suffolk.

A 60-minute video, demonstrating the principles and techniques described in this
book, is now available. For further details, send a stamped, addressed envelope
to: 'Training the Dog in the Human Pack', Greengarth, Maddox Lane, Bookham,
Surrey, KT23 3HT.

This book is dedicated to
the future of dog training

Its publication also coincides with my parents' 50th wedding anniver-sary. I hope that the message within these pages will be discussed by dog people around the world; if so, the world will have the oppor-tunity to hear about my parents.

They were sometimes hard to understand—or was that me?
They were sometimes unpredictable—or was that me?
They were sometimes totally unreasonable—or was that me?
But they were always there for me through all my ups and downs.

Their relationship has been a very special one, and now, so many years on, I can bask in the security of the love which they reflected.

My Dad has always taught me, 'if you believe in something, go for it', and this is what I have done in this book. His forthright 'speak your mind' attitude has certainly rubbed off on me, but we have both been fooled—we are as we are because my Mum allowed us to be.

As an author, I appreciate the unique opportunity given to me to be able to broadcast my beliefs. I have done just that in *Dogwise*—and proved them. I have also taken the liberty of abusing that opportunity to commemorate my Mum and Dad's very special occasion.

My personal message to them is, I love you both very much; to the rest of the world, who have never met George and Louise Fisher, they are just like the parents you love—plus a bit.

CONTENTS

LIST OF ILLUSTRATIONS

ACKNOWLEDGEMENTS

I would like to thank the following people who helped to make this book possible:

The Wood Green Animal Shelters and their staff at Godmanchester for allowing us to have Major in the first place, together with the photographs of their magnificent facilities.

Tony Glue for his wonderful ability to photograph dogs; it takes a GSD man to capture both the mood and the movement.

My friend Jill Holness whose ability to whizz around a word processor saved me hours of work; my only comment about her type-writing skills is that she needs all ten fingers, whilst I can type with just two.

My thanks also to go Hilda Mummery who allowed Daisy, her cute Westie puppy, to appear on the front of the jacket with Major.

Naturally, I thank Major for being such a wonderful dog, but special thanks must go to his handler, Robert Cox.

Thank you, Robert. Your good humour and equal determination to prove that dogs do not have to be punished in order for them to learn made working with you a pleasure.

Finally, I thank my wife Liz who encouraged me to continue on the same path, despite the pressure that we had no proof that the Home Office standard could be reached other than the traditional way.

The extract from *Don't Shoot the Dog* (Copyright © 1984 by Karen Pryor) is reprinted by permission of the author. The extract from *Training Your Dog: The Step-by-Step Manual* by Joachim Volhard and

1

THE EXPERIMENT

For many years now I have been quite forthright in my views that dog training is out of date.

There are many genuinely concerned dog owners who regularly attend dog training classes and religiously practise what they have been told to do, but still find that they have no control over their dogs when visitors arrive, or in the presence of other dogs, or when children are about. Some dogs, who behave perfectly within a class situation, still pull on the lead, jump up at the owners when they return home, run off when they are let off the lead, defecate, urinate, howl and bark when they are left, or become destructive in the owners' absence. All this, despite the fact that the owners are regularly drilling their dogs in the heelwork, sit stay, down stay and retrieve exercises that are taught within a class situation.

This book is about the successful training of a ten-month-old German Shepherd Dog called Major, using a completely reward-based programme, and explains how this approach can be used to train your own dog.

It follows Major's progress from his selection, through his training to the equivalent of the Home Office Police Dog standard; at the same time it relates the way he was trained to the training of the pet dog. Major was handled by Robert Cox, a dog handler with the City of London (Hampstead Heath Dept). (The Hampstead Heath dog section is not connected to the City of London Police Dog section; under an Act of Parliament the police have no powers on the Heath except by invitation or in pursuit.)

My copy of the Home Office Manual, *Police Dogs, training and care*, was written in 1963, but the current manual is almost exactly the same. The photographs are more up to date and the words 'choke chain' have been replaced by 'check chain', but the methods of training have not changed. I cannot think of any other area, be it medicine, child care or education, that has not advanced over recent years. Certainly there is a wealth of new knowledge available on training techniques and particularly on dog behaviour, but in general, when it comes to training dogs this new knowledge is not being utilised properly. The following extract nicely sums up what the Home Office Manual suggests the handler's attitude should be towards training his dog.

> Complete control is the groundwork on which all succeeding training is based. The successful teaching of obedience is brought about by a series of repetitive habit-forming exercises.
>
> The dog from the first day of training must never be allowed to ignore a command or fail to complete one given. The dog must never be allowed to suspect that there is even the possibility of being able to avoid a command. It is for this reason that training in all exercises must be commenced when the dog is restrained on the leash and therefore can be instantly guided into the action required. At the commencement of training the word of command may be accompanied by physical influence.
>
> Disobedience must be met with firmness.
>
> The use of physical punishment should only be resorted to in cases of emergency, and under no circumstances should it ever be considered a training measure. Proper use of the check chain, the verbal command or admonition and the withholding of praise are usually sufficient correctives.

It would be hard for anyone to disagree with these principles, but it is my belief that by following them we are expressing the attitude '*me human, you dog—I say, you do*'. Of course, that is our ultimate aim, but by adopting this stance at the commencement of training we risk causing resentment and resistance. If the dog responds in either of these ways, then he is not learning what we are trying to teach him. If we are trying to express our dominance over him by making him walk to heel—at the same time as teaching him what the word 'heel' means—then we are expecting him to learn two different concepts in one. The more the dog resists or resents the handler's dominant actions, the firmer those actions will have to be, and the more physical the training method becomes, the less will the dog enjoy the exercise.

We also run the risk of being unsuccessful in our initial attempts to influence the dog's actions by physical means. To a dominant dog, this would show that we had entered into a test of strength and had lost it, which would effectively demote the human and promote the dog. We would then be embarking on an uphill battle to form the proper partnership.

Police Dog training techniques are not the only ones in use, but I have taken them as an example of what I feel is wrong with traditional methods for a number of reasons:

1   In Major's case I was given the opportunity to train a handler and dog to Police Dog standard from scratch.

2   The standard required can be quantified: at the end of the training the handler and dog are assessed by two independent examiners.

3   It gave me the chance to throw away the accepted manual and use different techniques, based upon more scientific learning principles and a greater awareness of the instinctive behaviour of the dog; yet I felt I could still achieve, and indeed surpass, the required level of efficiency.

The very high standard required by the police is what most pet owners would regard as the ultimate in dog training. Guide dogs for the blind, hearing dogs for the deaf, sniffer dogs, mountain rescue dogs and others like them are more specialist areas which do not really relate to how people view dog training. The Police Dog who comes when called, stays when told to do so, walks to heel, is friendly unless threatened but whose aggression can be controlled is what most owners would want from their pet dog. By showing that different techniques can achieve this same standard and that these techniques can be applied to the everyday pet dog (except the more specialist areas of criminal work training), I hope I have proved the case for a radical change in the way dogs are generally trained in this country today.

I do not dispute the fact that the majority of dogs on a Home Office dog training course reach the required standard within the time allowed; I do know, however, that quite a number are rejected as unsuitable, and one of the reasons for this, which would not be shown on the rejection report, is the rigorous and physically dominating nature of the training techniques. This is also one of the reasons why some dogs do not respond to the training techniques still employed by many of the less forward-thinking dog clubs.

I was convinced before I began working with Robert and Major that a dog could be trained to a very high standard without the use of force. To do this required some radical changes in the techniques which are traditionally employed, and what these changes were will become evident as I describe the progress of the training programme. By far the most important change was in the attitude of the handler towards his dog.

I therefore had a goal to aim for and a hypothesis to prove: that dogs can be trained to any standard using a motivational and reward-based regime, as opposed to a corrective or punishment-orientated programme. In this book I have concentrated on the practical aspect of training your dog, which means that he does not pull on the lead, he comes back when you call and, in general, he acts in a socially acceptable manner; anything else you decide to teach him is icing on the cake. The emphasis throughout is on attitude—not only your dog's attitude towards you as the leader, but also your attitude towards your dog's ability to understand what you want him to do. In effect, I have tried to get you to accept your dog for what he or she really is—a domesticated animal with inherent pack and wild survival instincts, which learns in exactly the same way as all forms of intelligent life: if he finds an action rewarding, he will do it again; if it is not rewarding, he won't do it again. The first part of the book is therefore about understanding your dog; the mechanics of training come later.

What follows describes how we went about it, and our methods can be applied to any dog. What we did with Major, you can do with your dog, and you will discover that the experiment proved far more than I ever expected. Dog training really is easy—providing you understand the dog, its relationship with us, and how all animals learn.

2

THE MODERN DOG

As a direct descendant of the wolf, the modern dog exhibits something like 85 to 90 per cent wolf behaviour. Some behaviours are different, as a result of thousands of years of domestication, but as far as training is concerned, the differences are not an issue. The wolf and therefore the dog is a creature of instinct, a pack animal who views other members of his pack in terms of rank relevant to himself. Those above him he respects and obeys, those below him he does not—it is very much a black and white concept. Contrary to popular opinion, this rank structure is rarely achieved through aggression. Wolves are predators who hunt in packs; if they themselves are injured, they are unable to hunt, if they injure a member of their pack, the effectiveness of the hunting unit is reduced. Therefore rank is achieved mainly through taking and being allowed to take certain privileges. If we observe the behaviour of two dogs, we can see how quickly a rank structure is established; sometimes it can happen so quickly that we may miss the signs. One dog might hold its head high as it approaches the other. If the other lowers its head and averts any initial eye contact, they have established a dominance/submission level. This is occasionally established in a matter of seconds, without aggression or long drawn-out rituals.

With two fairly equal-ranking dogs, the procedure may take longer but again aggression is rarely involved. They might both compete over ownership of a stick, which we would interpret as playing together; but the dog that ends up with the stick will have emerged as the higher ranking. Further observation of these dogs will show that the higher ranking will lead and the other will follow—see how quickly one dog has taught the other to walk to heel.

The lower rank will hang back slightly when a narrow opening is approached to allow the higher rank through first—see how quickly the stay has been taught. In fact, many of the exercises that we attempt to train a dog to perform will happen naturally if we can establish the right dominance/submission level between us and the dog; all we then need to do is smarten up the behaviour, which is different from making the dog perform the behaviour in order to achieve this rank structure.

REVERSE APPROACH

Rather than starting the training of Major with continual bouts of heelwork training, I worked on establishing the right attitude from the dog towards Robert. It was my belief that this would result in our achieving the desired results on a non-confrontational basis, effectively removing any obstacles that might hinder the learning process. How this rank structure was achieved will be discussed as we observe how Major behaved over the course of the programme—what he did, why he did it and how we overcame any problem area. Many of the things we did might seem to bear no relevance to our final goal, but in fact they had the greatest influence on how Major learned. In effect, we ignored the formal side of the initial training and worked instead on the attitude. In the past it has been the accepted training technique to insist on the formal so that the attitude will eventually be influenced.

In my usual everyday work as a canine behaviour counsellor, I often have to explain to people that the reason why their dog bites visitors or chases joggers or attacks other dogs is because it thinks it has the right to do so. In other words, the problem that led their vet to refer them to me is not the real problem—it is the symptom. The real problem is that the dog has got the wrong idea about its role within the family pack.

Restructuring life in the den (at home) invariably overcomes the problem; after all, dogs bite and defend territory—this is normal canine behaviour. If the owners promote their dog to the rank of alpha animal, then the decision when and whom to bite rests with the dog.

From my work I know how effective rank restructuring can be when overcoming unacceptable behaviour, and my contract to train the City of London (Hampstead Heath) dogs gave me the opportunity to apply these techniques to a formal training situation. I hope my results will persuade people that the oldfashioned 'push-pull' techniques are not necessary any more, that they may indeed hinder the learning process and the eventual performance.

It is an interesting fact that scientists have studied dog behaviour and related a lot of it to the behaviour of young children—their competitiveness, their attention-seeking, their dominant gestures, which will include trophying the best (or in human terms, the most expensive) article, or squabbling over who sits in a particular chair; but although their findings have created a new understanding of how we should handle and teach children on a non-punitive basis, few people have ever reversed these findings back to the dog. Observation of human teenage behaviour will show many of the traits which are evident in the dominant dog. Parents of teenagers will have noticed pushy, almost aggressive behaviour: the increased occurrence, when passing them in doorways, of a noticeable reluctance to give way; a dislike of being seen to be familiar or to join in any family fun unless it is at their instigation. These are classic behaviours which are also noticeable in the dominant dog. I am not suggesting that all teenagers behave this way—but nor are all dogs dominant.

The more we learn about human behaviour, the more changes we initiate in teaching practices, motivational training and working conditions. Industry is probably at the forefront of some of the revolutionary ideas that are being introduced to create a more efficient workforce. At the same time, we are learning more and more about understanding dog behaviour; yet with the exception of a few more enlightened people, our training techniques are not keeping pace with this new knowledge. It is time we got up to date!

As you will see, the basic formula to which we shall be working is simple and one that can be applied to any dog:

1   First ensure that your dog sees you as the leader, but you must do this on a canine level. In effect, understand how the dog recognises and establishes dominance/submission levels and

apply these values instead of trying to get the dog to understand human values.

2 Having established the *right* to give an instruction, make sure the dog knows the meaning of the word and *wants* to perform the necessary actions. This requires a motivational approach, not a punishment-orientated approach.

The following pages will enable you to plan your own training programme for your dog. The techniques are not tied to any fixed time scale; each stage or exercise should be clearly understood by the dog before you move on to the next, and how long this takes is dependent upon the time you have available and your dog's own individuality.

It is a very straightforward and a very fair way to train your dog: if you don't want it to bark on command—don't teach it; if you don't want it to retrieve—don't teach it. The whole idea of the book is to help you to understand *how* to train your dog, rather than to preach 'this is what you must do'. After all, surely the definition of a 'trained dog' is a dog that does what you want it to do.

Using the techniques which I shall describe, you can improve your relationship and the behaviour of your dog without having to resort to chains around its neck, or physical punishment. I cannot stress enough that all you really need is to *understand* your dog and then use your common sense.

(Throughout the book I shall refer to choke chains, rather than check chains. I realise that when used correctly they are supposed to check the dog's forward progress. In my experience, the majority of people do not use them correctly and therefore they choke.)

IS TRAINING THE ANSWER?

I was recently sent a new publication for my comments, with a title suggesting that this was going to be a *new* guide to dog training. Within the first few pages it was showing the proper way to put a choke chain on a dog and where to place one's feet when 'giving it a firm jerk'. There were drawings of footprints all over the place and arrows showing which way to pull and which way to push to get the dog to perform certain movements. There were cartoon-like draw-ings of people and dogs going round in circles, and of people running backwards, pulling their dogs towards them on a lead. The circles depicted heelwork training, the figures running backwards were supposed to be teaching a recall. I have to admit that as I looked at these drawings I thought: 'Of course they won't pull—there's no-where to go if you are walking a circle—and they have to come back to the handler on a recall, they have no other option.' I am not suggesting that these methods will not eventually work with some dogs, but they certainly are not *new* and, in my opinion, they are not what the average pet owner wants or needs to do.

Most television programmes about training dogs, although effec-tive in making people more aware of the importance of having their dog trained, usually only touch the surface in relation to a dog that is living within a human pack. The problem that I now face in my work as a canine behaviour counsellor is that, because of these popular television programmes, the general dog-owning population now thinks that the answer to all a dog's anti-social behaviour is to have the dog trained. In the majority of cases, this is not sufficient.

The simplistic methods of training demonstrated in the pro-grammes suggest that all the average pet owner has to do is buy a dog, buy a choke chain to fit the dog, teach it some basic exercises like stay, sit and come, and life will be hunky dory—without doubt, this is how it comes over on television. This magical approach towards controlling dogs has convinced dog owners that all problems can be solved through training.

Training kennels have been set up that charge anything up to £500 to board and train your dog. When the owner arrives to collect it, he or she sees a demonstration of what the dog has been taught to do and for a little while (usually just a few days) this taught obedience transfers back to the dog's familiar environment. But in many cases this training is no different from the training that the dog receives within a club environment—putting it bluntly, the person handling the dog has ultimate control within the location in which the dog is being controlled; take the dog away from that location and remove the trainer, and the owner is right back to square one, but £500 poorer.

Of course it is important that a dog should be trained to respond to certain key words of command and, as dog owners, we have a responsibility to ensure that our dogs act in an acceptable manner towards visitors in the house and to strangers outside.

It is encouraging to see that more and more pet owners are rejecting the use of choke chains as a training aid and using more humane methods of control like head-collars, but in reality we are only using kinder methods to achieve the same result—that of teaching the dog to perform a trick: *heel, come, don't jump up, sit.*

We are now in a situation where the average pet owner is increasingly aware of his or her duty to own a well trained dog. There is a swelling anti-dog lobby, which has now reached the point where it has become a political platform to attract more votes, resulting in new legislation that imposes more controls over certain breeds. Meanwhile the media have been exploiting the situation for all its worth, thereby making dog owners even more anxious about their pet's behaviour. With the public having been almost brainwashed over the years into accepting the fact that training is the key to owning a well-behaved dog, there has been an upsurge of people seeking a training approach to their problems—but is it helping with the problems that we face today? In my opinion, it is not!

IS BEHAVIOUR THERAPY THE ANSWER?

Behaviour therapy for pets is becoming a trendy 'in thing' to be involved with. Without doubt it is a growth industry as more and more people, especially vets, discover the advantage of being able to refer their clients on to somebody who will give a one-to-one consultation with an owner, to enable him to understand and be able to control the behaviour of his dog. Even though I am involved with this growth industry, I am becoming concerned that a lot of people may see it as a short cut approach to owning a well-behaved dog. We cannot blame the vets for this: with a waiting-room full of patients, if the owner mentions that his dog would like to eat the postman, they just do not have the time to explain desensitisation programmes for that particular problem. If they know of someone who can do this on their behalf and on a professional level, they will refer the case on.

I am quite happy to see these cases on behalf of the vet and to report my recommendations back to him or her, but one of the questions to which I increasingly receive a negative answer is, what formal training programme have you done with the dog? If the answer is positive (dog club, private trainer or previous experience with dogs) I know that the owner has attempted to control the dog in general, even if on occasion the methods used have made the problem worse. But to hear that nothing has been done about teaching the dog to obey basic commands, and then have the owner complaining about a behaviour which has grown to problem level, suggests to me that there is no real commitment on the part of the owner towards his dog. Of course I shall still accept the case, but alongside the behaviour modification programme which I shall advise, there will be a suggestion to seek help with overall control. It is at this stage that I myself have a problem.

Although there is a growing number of clubs that use more enlightened and force-free methods of training, there are still a great many that cling to the oldfashioned stomp and yank techniques. I freely admit that hundreds of dogs have been successfully trained using these methods; on the other hand, hundreds of dogs have been ruined by them. To use a standardised training regime for every dog, regardless of its breed or temperament, does more harm than good. Dogs cannot be trained in such a way that they conform to an ideal pattern, and nor can their owners.

I think the time has come for us to face the fact that, over the last few years, some radical changes have taken place in the relationship between man and dog. For over 10,000 years the man/dog association has remained fairly consistent, with the dog being used either as an aid to man or a companion to him, but always treated as a dog. Around the time of the First World War, the training of dogs started to become standardised and recorded in training manuals and, except for slight variations in techniques and ideas, dogs could be successfully trained using the advice on offer. It is this advice that still forms the basis of most modern approaches to training—so why am I suggesting that it needs altering now if it has been successful for so long? It needs altering because our relationship with the dog has altered.

We only have to look at old photographs or paintings which show the family dog either in his basket in the kitchen or, if it was really spoilt, curled up at his master's feet in the living-room beside a roaring fire. Modern photographs will show the dog's bed in the master bedroom, but the dog is probably curled up on the master's bed. They may show the dog in the living-room, but if the master is in one armchair, the dog will be in the other; what you won't see is the roaring fire. It is not all that many years ago that the standard form of heating in most houses was by coal fire. As such, the dog's freedom of movement was restricted to access allowed by the human family member, as doors were kept shut to contain the heat.

Today, most homes are centrally heated and, with this form of heating, we have developed an open-plan style of living, giving freedom of movement around the house to the family dog. It is only in recent years that the average working family has become more affluent, and this affluence is on the increase as more and more people become home owners. A recent report suggested that in just a few decades, as parents pass on their property to their sons and daughters, there will be a wealth explosion. What this means is that we no longer regard our furniture or carpets as items that will have to last us for years and years; they are now disposable assets and we are not so protective of them as to deny the dog the right to enjoy them also.

There has also been a noticeable swing in the pattern of buying dogs. It used to be that couples had children and then bought a dog to complete the ideal family. Today, couples are very career-conscious and work hard in order to be able to afford the best of everything before deciding to have children. It is not unusual therefore for couples to get a dog, and quite often two dogs so that one will keep the other company whilst they are out at work. In the absence of children, these dogs are sometimes treated as child substitutes and their doting owners, who often feel quite guilty about leaving them during the day, overcompensate for this while they are at home.

The type of dog that is chosen today has also changed, with more people owning pedigree dogs which are often totally unsuited to the environment in which they are housed. Many of these have been bred to perform a specific task, like herding, guarding or hunting, but

THE MODERN DOG 15

because they look good, or reflect the owner's lifestyle, they are expected to become family pets and are housed under circumstances which provide no stimulation for their inherent instincts.

Commercial convenience petfood is now readily available, with added ingredients for healthier dogs and increased vitality. As top breeder and journalist Kay White commented recently, we are now feeding dogs with food fit for athletes, but not allowing them an athletic existence.

It is true that we try to give our dogs the best, usually prompted by the advertising claims of the petfood manufacturers, but if we are going to feed them on high quality proteins with the right amount of essential vitamins and minerals, we must allow them to burn them off with the right amount of stimulative on and off lead exercise. Generally, however, we do not. Another factor which is directly linked to our increased affluence is that the majority of dog owners also own a car and sometimes two, the second one being bought specifically with the dog in mind. It is easier to put the dog in the car and drive it to the local park for its daily exercise. It is not unusual for a client to tell me that his dog is not good on a lead because it rarely wears one.

These are just some of the major changes that have taken place in a relatively short space of time, all of which have a direct influence on the pet dog's behaviour. The area where the greatest effect is taking place is the way the dog views its role within the environment. If we are going to increase the dog's privileges by allowing it unrestricted freedom of movement and access to all parts of the house on demand, then we are making it think that it holds a far higher rank than even we do. If this is how the dog sees life, when we try to make it do something that it doesn't want to do, it will refuse or even aggressively object.

A COMBINED APPROACH

To summarise, it is my opinion that dogs used to respond quite well to the physical methods of training which became standard practice, but this was because they accepted our superior rank thanks to the way we lived with them. It is also my opinion that they would have responded even better to some of the more enlightened methods of today.

These physical methods no longer work as well because they create confrontation. On the one hand we are pushing, pulling and punishing wrong behaviour, whilst on the other hand, without realising it, we are doing everything possible to raise the status of the dog—obviously a lower rank should not tell a higher rank what to do.

Today, the knowledge is available to teach us how to apply more scientifically based, force-free methods for training any animal (including humans), but what is missing when it comes to a pack animal like the dog is the correct establishment of rank. We need to recognise that the majority of modern dogs are exhibiting problem behaviours directly linked to our modern way of life. If we can sort out the pecking order by simply restructuring the environment in which the dog lives with us, sometimes denying it several of the privileges that it has come to expect as its right, or by at least making it earn one or two of them, then we are half-way towards having a trained dog. All that is left is to teach it what we mean by our words and signals, and if we can do this in such a way that the dog enjoys obeying our commands, it is going to learn faster.

This is what this book is all about—linking behaviour therapy for problem dogs to training. I have become more and more concerned recently that 'dog training' and 'dog behaviour' seem to be splitting into two different disciplines. There are trainers who 'pooh-pooh' the behavioural approach to problem-solving, sticking to the principles that there is no such thing as a bad dog, only a bad owner, and that correct training will overcome the problem. There are people practising behaviour therapy who reject the training approach in favour of the purely scientific approach and the use of gadgets which are designed to prevent a problem occurring. What we should be doing is working together with one common aim—well-behaved, socially acceptable dogs.

It is all very well to sit down in front a keyboard and write what could well amount to an interesting theory. I have the confidence to write it, because when dealing with the behaviour problems of some of the dogs that are referred to me, I often advise the owner on how to improve his general control over the dog in tandem with the programme which I have advised to overcome the problem presented. In a recent survey which I conducted for the Association of Pet Behaviour Counsellors, of which I am a member, I found that 55 per cent of the cases referred to me had undergone some kind of formal training.

When I looked at aggressive behaviour only, I found that 72 per cent of the dogs had undergone formal training and most of the owners had arranged to 'train' them or have them 'trained' because of their aggression. Surely it must raise the question: if training works, why are the dogs still aggressive?

I know that the techniques I have advised in the past have worked because of the positive feedback received from my clients, but in almost all these cases the owner has first had to overcome the dog's suspicion of previous punitive training experience. With Major, a totally untrained dog, I had the opportunity for the first time to test my theory of dog training on virgin territory—by establishing a rank structure and then teaching the dog to respond in a certain way to a given command, without punishment for the wrong behaviour.

If, through writing about the results, I can at least get people to question the negative and forceful approach towards dog training which is still widely practised today, I shall feel that I have made a serious contribution towards a better understanding of the man/dog relationship. In view of the current anti-dog hysteria (which is hopefully at its height at the time of writing), anything that helps us appreciate why dogs behave in the way they do, and how easily they can learn if we use the right teaching techniques, can only help to improve matters in the future.

3

THE SELECTION

Before I describe why we chose Major, perhaps it would be a good idea to take a long, hard look at your own dog. Before any attempt is made to train him, you should make sure that you are thoroughly aware of his general attitude. Major will provide an example of the temperament and attitude of a young adult, and if your particular dog is within the 'young upstart' age bracket, you might look again at the points I made in the previous chapter about the similarity between dominant dogs and teenage humans: if your dog's normal behaviour is of a kind that you would not tolerate from a teenage human, then you should not tolerate it from your dog.

ASSESSING YOUR DOG

If you are contemplating buying a puppy, character assessments are extremely important. It should go without saying that you need to see the puppy with its mother, litter brothers and sisters. If this is not possible, then you should very seriously consider the breeder's reason for refusing this—and be suspicious. A good breeder will have no objection to this—and I stress the word 'breeder', not 'dealer'.

Ideally, you should be buying a puppy between the ages of seven and nine weeks. At seven weeks of age the genetic dominance/ submission potential of the puppy can be assessed by an experienced person. Having done this, a good breeder should be able to match the right type of dog to the right environment. All too often, my clients tell me that their dog picked them because he rushed forward and jumped all over them whilst the rest of the litter hung back. What they are saying is that this was probably the most dominant puppy in the litter, who had just made the first decision in their relationship together. This is fine if you are looking for a dominant character to do the sort of work Major was eventually able to do, but to place this sort of dog into the average family, with 2.2 children and a heavy mortgage which requires a lot of time at work to pay off, is very irresponsible of the breeder. Unfortunately, a lot of dogs become problems because they are not carefully placed in the right home and end up being put down at an early age (figures show that the most common cause of death in dogs under one year old is euthanasia because of a behaviour problem).

Whenever the word 'dominance' is mentioned it seems to conjure up pictures of aggression, but we should be careful not to confuse the two. It is very likely that a dominant dog will resort to aggressive behaviour if his dominance is threatened, but in many cases the owners do not recognise the significance of their dog's actions and so never challenge them. For example, they may believe that the dog likes to lie in a doorway because it is cooler, whereas the dog is probably displaying the fact that he controls that doorway. Many owners, when I ask if their dog likes to get on their beds or chairs, will tell me that he is not allowed to. I gently remind them that the question was, does he get on them, not, is he allowed to do so? In the case of dominant dogs, the answer is almost invariably yes, with the added comment that he knows he shouldn't be on them because he slinks off as soon as they enter the room. What we are talking about here is what I call passive dominance: the dog never shows any signs of objecting to the rules being enforced, but in fact he breaks them at every opportunity. If he was not in any way 'pushy' in his attitude and was not allowed on the furniture, he wouldn't get on it, it is that simple. The fact that he keeps trying should tell the owner a lot about his basic attitude.

Submissive types rarely present problems to their owners and are generally easy to assess and, because there is no need to establish rank, much easier to train. There is one exception to this rule and that is the dog that is psychologically dominant but physically submissive. This type of dog will still break the rules, but when you reprimand him for doing so he will roll over on his back or submissively urinate. In these (fairly rare) cases, the dog has learnt that displays of submission will stop further hostile behaviour on the part of the owner—it is called 'trained submission'.

We can easily recognise the extreme ends of this dominance/submission spectrum, but it is the grey areas in between that we need to study and assess. With a puppy you can write your own rules from day one, but in the case of an older dog you should spend a few days studying his daily routine and the things that he does ritualistically (on a regular basis). If our dogs are doing the same things regularly, then somehow or other they are being rewarded for them, or there is a purpose to them. Some of these things might not create a problem for us, but if we want to understand the dog better we need to know why he does them. For example, when the family is sitting down watching TV, does the dog go and lie out in the hallway? This is not something which we would consider a problem, but from where he lies, does he get the best view of every room and can anyone go from one room to another without the dog seeing them? If the answer is yes, he does do that, and no, we cannot move without the dog seeing us, then perhaps he is lying in the hallway because this is the best vantage point for surveying his pack, as well as guarding his territory. This might or might not indicate how he sees his role within the pack structure. On its own it is not particularly indicative of anything, but it is a different behaviour from the more submissive type who would tend to curl up at the feet of its owner and go to sleep.

Take careful note of how the dog greets you in the morning. Does he come to you with his tail wagging slightly and carried low, head held low and ears slightly back? Or does he look up from his bed and wait for you to go and pat him before he decides to get up? These are the things we should be looking at, the type of daily occurrence to which we rarely give a second thought. It is amazing how many times I am given an immediate answer to a question about the dog's routine, only to find that, on reflection, what they thought was happening was not what was happening at all.

Before we can start to train a dog to be a well-behaved member of the family unit, we must really understand what his attitude is towards everyone within that unit. Careful observation is the only way to do this and sometimes what we see, instead of what we think we see, can prove very revealing. It pays dividends to discuss the dog's attitude with everyone who is regularly involved with him and see how they assess him: you may find that although he appears to be submissive to you, he is dominant towards others.

Establishing where the dog sees his role within your pack structure can be an eye-opening exercise to most families. Ask, for example, how the dog greets each and every member of the family when they return home. If he greets them all in the same way, he is either submissive or dominant depending on the manner of greeting. If there is a variation in the greeting procedure, then the dog sees his role as somewhere in between and this is something that you should be aware of.

ASSESSING MAJOR

Choosing a dog that is suitable material for police-type training can take time. We needed a dog that was physically capable of performing the tasks required, was of the right temperament (confident and outgoing), and would be keen to involve him- or herself in play with the prospective handler. Of course, rearing a puppy that has been selectively bred, puppy walked and puppy trained is the ideal situation, but this was not possible under the circumstances. We needed a young adult that was ready for training straight away.

The selection of handlers for this type of work is just as important, and although I was not involved in Robert's selection, in my opinion he perfectly met the criteria necessary for a good dog handler. To a certain extent, what we look for in the dog we should also look for in the handler, and Robert possessed all of these qualities.

Robert was 26 years old and although not married—which is usually one of the main considerations for selection—he was nevertheless in a stable relationship which offered the consistent and responsible environment essential if a firm bond was to be established between dog and man.

He was an experienced handler, in that he had worked an operational dog for four years, but unfortunately the dog had had to be retired because of hip displasia—a malformation between the hip ball and socket joints which can make even walking an extremely painful experience for some dogs.

Robert's ability to do the job had been proven; from my point of view—considering the fact that I would have to work with him for twelve weeks—it came as a great relief to find that he also had the type of personality which made the working relationship between us enjoyable. I did, however, learn one thing about him, and that was never to tell him a joke. If I did, the rest of the session would be interspersed with the most excruciatingly corny jokes from him, which just seemed to go on and on. From what I learned during our conversations, it was a good job that there was no karaoke machine on the training field—I would never have been able to prise the microphone out of his hands.

It is just this sense of humour (debatable in Robert's case) and the extra confidence required to be able to act the fool in front of an audience, just for the fun of it, that separates the man who becomes a dog handler from the man who works with a dog.

I shall always be indebted to the staff of Wood Green Animal Shelters at Godmanchester, Cambridge, who, having heard that I was on the look-out for a German Shepherd (male or female) around twelve months old, rang me to say that one had just been brought in for re-homing. It was a male, ten months old and too much for its owners to cope with. What too much meant was evident when Robert and I travelled to Godmanchester to see him. Major was huge and extremely active but with a kind expression which was probably enhanced by the fact that one of his erect ears tipped inwards towards the other—not exactly the ideal show dog but a fault which certainly gave him character. His owners were both professional people who just did not have the time to devote to his energy requirements or stimulation needs, and consequently he had become too much of a handful for them.

He was a very confident dog in a pushy sort of way. He liked to lean against you and would take every opportunity to grasp your hand in his mouth or playfully pull at your clothing. These behaviours, although on the face of it friendly gestures, were in fact very domi-nant traits. Leaning is a canine way of letting you feel the dog's strength, while hand, arm and clothing 'mouthing' are an invitation to play a competitive game of rough and tumble—it is high-ranking dogs that initiate play activity. He was very keen to chase and pull on any toy that was presented, but not keen at all to bring it back to you

Wood Green Animal Shelters, Godmanchester: the mushroom-style kennel blocks.

Staff with dogs in the play and exercise yard.

once he had managed to gain possession of it—another dominant possessive trait.

He was keen to spot movement without over-reacting to it and showed just the right amount of suspicion when taken towards someone who was acting in a strange manner (hiding behind an obstacle and withdrawing when spotted). His behaviour when he was taken towards other dogs was interesting to watch. He behaved initially as if they were not there and it was they who approached him. His body postures where all forward, whereas the approaching dogs were all back and low. There was absolutely no sign of aggression, but also no desire to associate with them. Obviously these dogs recognised his aloof attitude and did not push the issue; they obviously saw straight away what I was looking for, the ideal Police Dog material.

The most important aspect of selecting a dog for training had by now become clear—Robert liked him a lot. The bond between the handler and his dog is of the utmost importance. For sure, it can develop as the training progresses, but when it is there from the onset of the relationship it bodes well for a successful partnership. Anyone who admires the regal attitude of the German Shepherd Dog could not fail to appreciate Major's (all in proportion) size and obvious confidence, and it was evident that Robert had just met the dog that he could feel proud to be handling. But the curious thing was that Major appeared to like Robert as well; I suppose there is no accounting for tastes and there will always be certain aspects of canine behaviour that we will never understand.

There was now going to be a five-day settling-in period from selection to the start of training, during which Robert was instructed to take his new dog home and basically just feed, exercise, live with and observe him. A kennel had been set up in Robert's garden to house his dog, but I wanted him to be predominantly part of the family. Robert's family were to become Major's pack and he could learn nothing about the structure if he was isolated all the time in his kennel. By the same token, the kennel had been supplied to satisfy the City of London's legal responsibility to provide the handler with safe and secure premises to house his dog. Therefore it was important also that Major should not object to being kennelled. Making sure that the dog will accept isolation to the fringes of the den is one way of establishing a hierarchical structure, as well as following all the principles about how we now live with dogs, described in Chapter Two; but, if Major's training was to have any bearing on the training of the domestic dog, it was important that Robert should start to live with him on as near a pet dog basis as was practical. Making sure that he could be kennelled would be no different from making sure that the pet dog can occasionally be shut in the kitchen without complaining.

Robert understood perfectly that no initial attempts to teach Major were to be undertaken, other than the rules of his household. We had the advantage that it generally takes a dog a couple of days to adjust to a new environment and about 10–14 days before he starts to take advantage of the privileges which we might inadvertently grant him. With this in mind, Robert took Major home and, according to his report, Major very quickly showed that he was quite used to being granted privileges within the house. After his initial curiosity was satisfied by sniffing in every nook and cranny—in one of which he found Robert's cat who instantly swiped him across the nose to tell him who was boss—Major settled down on the settee. Robert took a leaf out of the cat's rule book: he unceremoniously dumped Major on the floor and sat on the settee himself. As I had suggested, a couple of days of spreading kitchen foil on the chairs stopped Major carrying on a habit which he had obviously learnt in his previous home. A baby gate erected at the foot of the stairs allowed access upstairs for the humans but denied Major—better to make it impossible for him to do things than to have confrontation by verbally or physically stopping him. Even exercise rules were laid out from day one: Major was taken to a spot in the garden and Robert waited for him to defecate (15 minutes on the first occasion); he was rewarded with a tit-bit and then taken for a walk. Teaching dogs this routine makes clearing up after them much easier and is fairer on non-dog owners. Even town or flat-dwelling dogs can be taught to defecate in one particular place before the walk commences, and this encourages them to 'hurry up'. Similarly, giving a small portion of their daily food ration when they return from the walk makes it worth being put back on the lead at the end of some free-running exercise and improves the recall.

Whilst all this was going on, I was looking forward to starting the course.

4

FIRST DAYS

Before Major started his training we had to have some structure to work to. To a certain extent this would be dictated by his progress, but at this stage there had to be some basic ground rules laid down. The first, and in my opinion the most important, was that for the next twelve weeks Robert, Major and myself would be working together on a daily basis. When dogs meet up, they quickly establish a pecking order—this is acceptable and natural behaviour which dogs understand. The first radical change in Major's training was that from day one he was going to understand that, of the three of us, he was number three. This understanding of where he stood in the pecking order would traditionally be a gradual understanding brought about through training, which, if you think about it, is totally alien to the way dogs usually behave.

Before we did this we needed to know what impact this change in the accepted (traditional) system would have on Major's progress. What better way than to look at the basic exercises that he would eventually have to perform, assess the areas where we might have difficulty so that we could work on them as a priority, establish a pecking order, and then reassess the basics to see if there had been an improvement?

At the end of his training he would be tested in the exercises listed overleaf, which had been slightly altered from the usual Police Dog tests to suit the requirements of the service in which he would work. The possible marks allocated to each exercise had also been altered, simply to make the judging easier, without losing sight of the fact that Major had to score a 70 per cent plus mark in every group.

OBEDIENCE

		POSSIBLE MARKS
Heel Free	Walking to heel	20
	Leaving dog in sit	5
	Leaving dog in down	5
	Leaving dog in stand	5
	Leaving dog in sit when marching	5
	Leaving dog in down when marching	5
	Leaving dog in stand when marching (calling dog to heel on direction)	5
	Retrieve	10
	Distant control finishing with recall	10
	Speak on command	10
	Down out of sight (5 minutes)	20
	TOTAL	100

AGILITY

	POSSIBLE MARKS
Hurdles	10
Long jump	20
Scale	20
(mark on control as well as agility)	
TOTAL	50

SEARCHING FOR PROPERTY

	POSSIBLE MARKS
4 Articles in square 12yds × 12yds	
5 minutes allowed	
20 marks for each article	
Handler not allowed in square	80
Retrieving buried article	20
TOTAL	100

	POSSIBLE
MAN WORK	MARKS
Searching for person	50
(mark for quartering and speaking)	
Crowd control	20
Test of courage (stick chase)	50
Chase (dogs will be required to be off the	
lead before 'chase' in the down position)	50
Marks will be given for control on 'leave'	
TOTAL	170

TRACKING	
Track to include at least 3 turns	80
TOTAL	80
POSSIBLE OVERALL MARKS	500

I shall describe these exercises in full detail at the relevant points in Major's training. At this stage we were testing for ability and willingness to perform the basics of the tasks which would eventually be required.

The basics required for Major to perform all the exercises were: Recall; Sit; Down; Stand; Retrieve; Heel on leash; Chase after a rag held by somebody; Track (follow a scent trail); Search (look for, by the human scent on it, a hidden article or toy).

The training area at this point was restricted to my home environment. Later on we would expand Major's experience to a very wide variety of locations. Initially we took him into my paddock (one third of an acre) which was escape proof. My office overlooked this paddock and that in itself was quite large (5m × 3.6m). Having allowed Major to investigate the surroundings, we gently put him through the basics, using both paddock and office, and recorded his reactions. At this point we were interested only in his ability to perform; we were not insisting that he perform the exercises correctly. This was another

Major's initial training area: (above) *the paddock and* (opposite) *the author's office. Both were escape-proof.*

radical change in the accepted methods—we did allow him to refuse, or not obey a command. The results were as follows:

RECALL (tested outside). Non-existent. He would look when he was called, but wag his tail, which he carried quite high, and the look on his face clearly said NO!

SIT (tested inside). Fair. He obeyed on the third command.

DOWN (tested inside). Non-existent. Of course, we could have made him, but that was not what we were looking for.

STAND (tested inside). Non-existent. Perhaps he had never been taught the meaning of the word. Again we could have made him, but at this stage we were testing his ability only.

RETRIEVE (tested outside). Non-existent. He was very keen to chase after and pick up the article, but when called went into his NO recall mode. If Robert ran away, he would drop the article and chase after him. Major made sure that Robert could not catch him and any move by Robert to walk towards where the article had been thrown resulted in Major picking it up and running off with it.

HEEL (tested outside). Non-existent. Major was being walked on a broad leather collar and insisted on being in front. Robert was instructed to check him back, but as soon as the pressure was released, Major forged ahead again. (I do know how to check a dog, but as I have made quite clear, we were not engaged in any training exercises at this stage).

RAGWORK (tested outside). Good. Having teased him with a tug-of-war game for the possession of a piece of sacking, I ran off with the trophy and he was more than willing to chase me and try to win it back. This boded well for his future criminal (man work) exercises.

TRACK (tested outside). Good. After teasing Major with a toy, I walked across the paddock, scuffing my feet along the ground as I went. This would release a ground scent that an interested dog could follow. I placed the article so that it could not be seen easily, returned along the same route and then distracted Major's attention for a few seconds. Then he was asked (whilst restrained on a collar and leash) to 'track'. He ran a few feet in the general direction, stopped, put his nose to the ground and followed the scent trail to the reward.

SEARCH (tested outside). Fair. Whilst Major was restrained on his collar and leash, I teased him with a small toy. The toy was thrown into the paddock (it was small enough not to be visible where it landed). Major was distracted by being turned round and then released in a different direction to 'find'. He was extremely persistent in his attempts to find the thrown article, which showed that his memory, olfactory (scenting) abilities, and dedication to the job in hand were fine. Once he had found the article, his NO recall/retrieve attitude took over.

In fact, what Major displayed during these 'assessment of abilities' tests was:

You have no right to herd me, or to call me back to the pack—THE RECALL.
I will sit because I have learnt that it suits me eventually—THE SIT.
I will not lie down, because that is a submissive posture—THE DOWN.
I do not understand the word 'stand' (not usually taught to pets)—STAND.
I will chase after and possess an article (it is now mine)—RETRIEVE.
I insist on my right to go first and precede all others—HEEL.
I want to own that rag and I will come and take it off you—RAGWORK.
I know you have hidden something and I want to possess it—TRACK.
I have seen you throw something which should be mine—SEARCH.

In effect, all his abilities to perform the tasks that would eventually be required of him were there; all we needed to do was channel them and put them under our control. From a behavioural point of view, this meant that we must express our right to certain canine privileges, without destroying the competitive spirit that should be evident in all good working dogs. As I have said, my hypothesis was that a sound knowledge of behaviour and an equally sound knowledge of training could work hand in hand to produce quicker and improved results.

Following this assessment, Major was brought into the office whilst Robert and I discussed the significance of his dog's behaviour. During this time, Major acted like an utter yob. He barked a lot, significantly straight into Robert's face. He paced up and down and constantly scratched at the door (I need a pee so badly). Having walked him round the paddock to establish that he didn't really need a pee, Robert was surprised to see that he continued this door-scratching behaviour within seconds of his return. I wasn't! His 'I will please myself' attitude on the training paddock was bound to be exhibited inside.

What was most significant about his general attitude, to my mind, was his predictable behaviour after he had been stroked, especially over the top of his head and along the withers: he would walk away and shake himself. When dogs are tracking (following the scent of a person) and reach a particularly difficult area where they find it hard to ascertain which scent to follow, they invariably stop, shake them-selves, and then continue, usually in the right direction. I had always assumed that what they were doing was shaking off any scent particles from their body hairs which the wind might be carrying towards their olfactory systems and which were confusing the scent they were trying to follow.

My APBC colleague David Appleby had noticed the same be-haviour when he used to train guide dogs for the blind. He noted that it usually occurred when a dog was trying to negotiate a particularly difficult obstacle, like trying to assess the clearance for the handler under some scaffolding. His diagnosis was that it was a stress reaction. My subsequent observations have been that I never see a submissive type of dog exhibit this behaviour after it has been stroked, but I often see a dominant character do so. Could it be that stroking the head, neck and shoulders (dominant regions of a dog) is depositing a scent on it which it does not accept? Or could it be that dogs who have attained a very high rank, which they are not genetically equipped to cope with, are under a great deal of stress? I do know that when I observe my own dogs play-fighting, the most dominant of them always shakes after the interaction has finished. If

two of them shake, the play-fight starts again. Whether this behaviour is a stress or a dominant reaction will be interesting to follow
up and both David and I have resolved to look at it more closely in the
future.

Major's attitude on the training field had told me a lot about his
attitude to life in general. His behaviour in my office was really an
extension of this same attitude. He wanted to take charge and it was
within this environment that the real training should begin; after all,
if we could not control him within a secure environment, we would
have no chance outside.

It is an interesting fact of life that the average pet owner views the
problems he has with his dog in terms of how the dog behaves
outside the home. Invariably he has the same problems inside, but
because they occur within closed and secure premises, they do not
create a problem. The owner drops some bacon rind on the floor, for
example, and calls the dog: no response. He calls again: no response.
He enters the room where the dog is asleep, calls it again and
encourages it to follow: some response. He guides the dog to the
fallen tit-bit and the dog gets rewarded, but the owner does not see a
problem. If you consider that every time we call our dogs indoors, it is
to reward them in some way—food on the floor, your dinner's ready,
I've got your lead in my hand—but rarely as a simple recall exercise,
then you might appreciate that when the dog is running free in the
park, rewarding itself with hunting, shooting and fishing games,
coming back to us to be put on a lead and taken home is a very
unrewarding activity. The fact that the dog does not come back when
on a walk is regarded as 'the problem', whereas the lack of response
indoors is explained away: the dog was asleep, it didn't hear because
it was in another room—in fact any excuse rather than face up to the
fact that the dog is not responding to an indoor recall. This is the real
problem but it is not regarded as such because the dog is contained
and therefore its refusal to obey does not create a problem for the
owner.

Having realised a long time ago that the root cause of the majority
of dominance-related behaviour problems stemmed from how the
dog saw its role within the pack, and mindful of what I said in
Chapter Two, that we may inadvertently promote the dog to a higher

rank simply by granting him privileges which, if he were a feral dog (domesticated turned wild) or a wolf, would be reserved for the highest ranking, I researched and developed a technique of using a 'sound' to control behaviour and establish some basic canine principles. The end result of this research was a training aid called 'Dog Training Discs'. The technique involved has been incorrectly used for many years by people who advocate throwing choke chains at the dog to give it the impression that 'it may be twenty feet away from the handler, but it can still be reached'. So far as I can ascertain, the first recorded advice (in a book) to throw something at the dog, be it a chain, a bunch of keys or a stick, was around 1910. Since then, trainers have used the 'casting chain or throwing stick' technique with great effect to cure recall problems. In a lot of cases, by following the advice laid down, it does work. It is suggested that when the dog is at a distance from the owner and completely distracted, a chain (or stick or bunch of keys) should be thrown at the dog without it knowing where it came from. The handler then calls the dog, who is quite happy to respond because it feels threatened from an unknown source. Without doubt, this technique has proved so successful that people have used it for years in one form or another, without questioning *why* it worked. I used it myself for many years with great success, even though half the time my aim was rotten and I missed the dog by miles, or just as I let go of the chain the dog turned round to look at me; but the end result was always the same: the dog came back to me.

Now this never did make sense to me. If I were a dog and I knew that someone was throwing things at me, I would be off in the opposite direction as fast as my four legs would take me; yet invariably, even though the dog sees where the missile is coming from, it returns to the launching pad. In 1984, quite by chance, I realised that the secret of this technique is the orientating effect of the sound: the dog's attention is diverted from what it was doing and becomes centred on the owner. As a result, I spent a long time researching the use of sound to interrupt unwanted behaviour, with great success. The only drawback at that time was that if the dog kept hearing the sound when it did not relate to its behaviour, then the initial effect of the technique would be lost. Having spent a long time trying things like chains, keys, or pebbles in a can, all of which work initially and are still used by many people, albeit incorrectly, I rejected these items and went in search of something more distinctive. I needed a sound unlike any other, and, I wanted to be able to pick up and put down whatever created the sound without making a noise, so that the dog only heard it at the exact moment of the unwanted behaviour. The answer was a series of brass discs which fit together but can be 'chinked' like castanets at the right moment, now called 'Dog Training Discs'.

The key to their success lies in the introductory conditioning procedure, which should be carried out away from the problem you want to cure. The reason for this is that the sound produces an increasingly negative effect, starting with barely an awareness of it and building very quickly to actually avoiding it. An analogy might be the effect on you of receiving a static shock from the car door. On the first occasion you take note; by the fourth or fifth occasion you have become acutely aware of what might happen and shut the door with your elbow. We therefore do not need to condition the dog when the problem is evident and the dog's concentration is fully distracted; it is quicker and more effective to heighten the dog's awareness under controlled conditions. This is something that the users of other sound-producing, often everyday items like a bunch of keys do not do—they simply throw or rattle the item whenever the dog is doing something to which they object. I recently heard about a dog that was bonked on the head with a tin can full of pebbles whenever it barked at another dog. It stopped the barking immediately which the owner thought was magic; the problem was that he could not walk the dog on the lead if he had the can in his pocket, because every time it rattled the dog lay down as if it was dodging bullets.

Over the years, more and more people who are involved in dog training and behaviour therapy have started to use the Discs, and as a result I have had a lot of positive feedback which has enabled me to understand how and why the system works. *Why* does it work? is a question that has been asked of me on countless occasions by clients who have just seen their dogs change from extreme hyperactivity to calm, relaxed, well-controlled pets in a little less than five minutes,

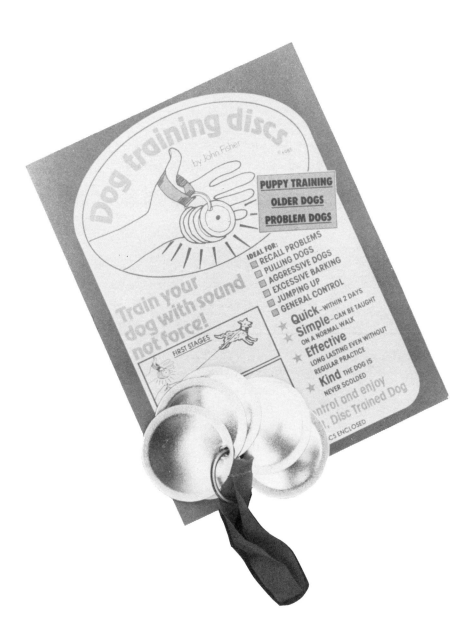

and with no shouting or negative physical contact. My answer has always been that I was not really sure. During the research period, I worked on a trial and error basis until I had developed what I thought was the most effective technique, but I admit that I did not fully understand *why* all the dogs, regardless of age, breed or temperament, responded in the same predictable manner. I am indebted to my APBC colleagues Peter Neville and Valerie O'Farrell for their scientific input and explanation of the Discs' effectiveness.

Together, they were tutoring a course in canine/feline behaviour to vets in Glasgow. Peter demonstrated the use of the Discs on three dogs, all of which responded in exactly the same way. Valerie, who had heard about the Discs but had never seen them used, watched this demonstration with interest. Her comment to Peter at the end of the day was the same as that of my clients: 'I can see it works, but *why?*'

As a result, two of the country's top behavioural psychologists spent the next five hours talking about all the known theories on how dogs learn. At one point, even Valerie's own dogs were conditioned to the Discs and they also responded in the same predictable manner. This conversation was followed by many weeks of field work and watching the dogs' reaction to the conditioning process. In the absence of any other explanation, they have concluded that the initial introduction preconditions the dog to an avoidance response whenever it hears that unique sound. Once the dog is 'tuned' in to the sound, it can then be used to interrupt the majority of unwanted behaviour patterns. From a behavioural point of view, it is best if the Discs are limited in their use to overcoming the major problems; this ensures that the dog does not become confused and the sound does not lose its effectiveness through over-use. But they can also be used to promote the rank of the owner and as an aid to training a dog, which is exactly why I wanted to use them with Major.

Briefly, the technique involves offering the dog something (like a tit-bit) from the hand and then, without saying anything to the dog, placing a tit-bit on the floor. The moment the dog goes to take it, the Discs are thrown alongside the food and the food is removed. Invariably, the dog ignores the Discs and continues to look for the food, but as far as we are concerned at this point, it can do what it likes. This procedure is repeated three or four times (more with some dogs, less with others).

Eventually, when the food is placed on the floor, the dog immediately backs away. Invariably, it goes and sits next to the owner, but if it is the owner who is introducing the Discs at home, it will go to its bed or some other favourite resting place. In Major's case, he went and sat beside Robert and stage one of introducing the Discs had been successful. From the dog's point of view, what is being established, at the same time as the sound is beginning to register, is: *you can have the food I give you and don't want, but do not step inside my personal space and take my food*. This is very much how one dog would trophy a bone from another and is a classic canine expression of rank.

To enhance the effectiveness of the Discs and increase the rank of the human over the dog, I usually move on to stage two—using the Discs in the doorway. In narrow openings (like doorways), while humans exhibit behaviour similar to that of dogs and wolves, our behaviour is a little more refined because we are supposedly more intelligent. If a high-ranking person is occupying a narrow opening and we need to go past, we say 'excuse me'. What we mean, of course, is, *I need to go past you but I don't expect you to move very far, it's just that I will try not to touch you*. If it is a lower ranking human in the doorway, we still say 'excuse me', but what we mean is, *I am coming through and if there is any physical contact, you have been warned*. Canine or lupine behaviour dictates that if a higher rank occupies a narrow opening, lower ranks do not approach until their passage is clear. Thinking back again to Chapter Two, look how much scope we are giving the domestic dog to express his rank within our modern open plan environment.

I approach the doorway without saying anything to the dog. As I open the door slightly, the dog (often out of habit) makes for the chink of light that appears. I drop the Discs and shut the door at the same time—without trapping the dog's nose, I hasten to add. Again, after three or four repetitions I should be able to stand in the open doorway, completely ignoring the dog who by this time should again be lying next to the owner (or back in his bed at home).

Not only have I further increased the effectiveness of the Discs, but

I have also established another rank privilege: *do not push past me through narrow openings.*

Although this is a pretty simplistic explanation of the Discs and how they are introduced, it should be understood that, although they are a form of aversion therapy, they are not an unpleasant aversion like electric shock therapy or hitting the dog or even, as some have described it, startling the dog, which the high-pitched whistles for dog control can do. If this were so it would be more effective the first time it was used, and this is very rarely the case. What happens (we think) is that the sound precedes the removal of the object that interests the dog, thereby frustrating its intentions. Eventually it realises that the sound means *you are wasting your time*, and at this point we can offer a more rewarding alternative, like praise from the owner, or food or a toy. In effect, we are giving a dog the choice: do this and see what happens (a waste of time and not nice); do this and see what happens (very rewarding and very nice). It is a pretty dumb dog that does not quickly learn to perform the more rewarding behaviour.

By giving choices, we are in fact asking the dog to think about what it is doing. This is a concept which is generally rejected by the traditional approach—dogs don't think, they just do what they have been conditioned to do. As the Home Office Manual states, 'The successful teaching of obedience is brought about by a series of repetitive habit-forming exercises.' By taking this view, we are creating problems for ourselves in that we 'condition' a dog to behave in a certain way under certain circumstances, which is entirely different from understanding what it should be doing. In distance control, for example, the dog is required to stand, sit, or down, on command from a distance. Many handlers will tell you that it is relatively easy to get the dog to stand from a sitting position, but not so easy to get it to stand from the down position. This is because it has not actually learnt the word 'stand', it has only learnt to stand from a sit on hearing the command—in other words, it has been conditioned to follow a routine, and if we use the same words out of sequence or away from the routine, it generally does not know what to do.

During the conditioning process of the Discs, first with the food and then with the door, there is a point just before the dog follows the predicted response of returning to the owner or going to its bed where it stands perfectly still, sometimes for a full minute and in some cases for longer.

Seconds before it makes the decision, its tail wags briefly (if it has one) and this indicates to me that it is about to do something. This does not occur with every dog, but it does with far too many for it to be a coincidence; the standing still would suggest to me a thinking phase, and the tail wag a decision phase. Obviously, grabbing the food off the floor or rushing at the open doorway is a conditioned action which the dog has done so many times in the past that the interruptive effect of the Discs creates a set of unfamiliar circumstances. The dog is forced to reconsider its actions and concentrate on what is happening.

A good example of this conditioned as opposed to considered action is to ask the handler of an obedience-trained dog to stand with the dog positioned by his right leg, instead of the usual left leg. Tell him to instruct the dog to 'sit'—and watch the dog scoot to the left and sit perfectly. I say 'scoot', because this is what most dogs will do, relieved that they are back into a familiar routine which they eventually learn to perform without having to think about it or concentrate on what they are doing. It is because dogs don't concentrate on what they are doing that problems arise, either in training or competing, when they miss out an obstacle on an agility round, or hit a jump which they could easily clear, or in the behavioural area when they automatically throw themselves at the door if the bell goes, even though they may know it is you on the other side. They are simply reacting to the circumstances without thinking about what they are doing.

Altering that routine, for instance making a trained dog walk on the right-hand side instead of the left, invariably has an instant, calming effect on an excitable dog and its body posture changes completely. This is because it is a new situation in which there is no familiar conditioned pattern to follow; the dog has to engage the brain, instead of just reacting to the circumstances. I have noticed with dogs which show aggression to other dogs—but only when they themselves are on the lead—that if you get the owner to hold his dog on his right side and then introduce another dog, it will rush to the left side before showing aggression. If he can manage to keep it on the right, it is less likely to do so.

Making sure that Major listened to the commands instead of going through conditioned routines was to be a feature of his training. The Discs would be useful to make him stop and think, or we would change the exercise slightly if it looked as though he was learning a routine instead of the meaning of a word. At this stage we did not know if we would need to do anything at all, but whilst he was learning we would have to be constantly aware exactly what he was learning.

His response to the Discs was classic and he immediately settled down and was noticeably more relaxed—an expected reaction in dogs who have just been relieved of their responsibilities, and something that I have recorded in my books *Think Dog* and *Why Does My Dog . . . ?* It was also noticeable that when Robert put on Major's lead to take him back to the van, he did not push past him in the doorway and he walked calmly (without pulling) all the way down the drive and across the car park. He was not at any time given instructions to heel or to wait.

Before taking him home, Robert and I again discussed the importance of expressing the rank of the human through the everyday interactions with the dog within the home.

The following day, we retested the basic exercises with the following results:

RECALL. Major's response was instant from a free running situation, when Robert called him he returned at once and very quickly. I was pleased to note that his ears were ever so slightly back and his head carriage not so high, a classic submissive but not fearful approach.

SIT, DOWN AND STAND. These were tested indoors again. The sit was instant: he allowed himself to be coaxed into a down (the day before he had gone rigid); he also allowed Robert to coax him into a stand (the day before he had become hyperactive, barking and jumping up).

RETRIEVE. Same enthusiasm to chase and pick up the article, but this time he brought it straight back to Robert and dropped it at his feet.

The Recall: Major's initial 'No' attitude. He looks up but does not move, and his head and tail are held high.

(Overleaf) The Recall: Major's 'Yes' attitude after rank restructuring. He responds immediately, running back to Robert with his head and tail held low.

HEEL. No attempt to pull, and even when Robert changed direction there was no need for physical influence; he followed with only slight coaxing.

SEARCH. Same enthusiasm and dedication. He picked up the article and responded straight away to Robert's call, dropped the article half-way and ran to Robert; on being sent back he relocated it and returned with it, this time giving it to hand.

These results exceeded my expectations: just two days into the training and we appeared to have overcome all the problem areas without any formal training, without any force and without using any negative methods directly connected to the exercise. The next stage would be to move on to the formal training. First, however, it might help you in training your own dog to gain some understanding of how dogs learn.

Dog Training Discs are available from:
Dog Training Discs, Greengarth, Maddox Lane, Bookham, Surrey KT23 3HT.

5

RECALL PROBLEMS

Let us assume that you have correctly assessed your dog and as a result have established a clear-cut pack structure in which, from your dog's point of view, you are in charge. The next stage is to teach him what you mean by certain words of command. Throughout this book I shall stress the importance of positive reinforcement as a training aid, and the biggest problem I have with 'dog people' is overcoming their reluctance to use food for this purpose. They are quite happy to use a toy as an incentive, which they don't regard as bribery, but food they do regard as bribery.

What I would ask at this stage is: if the dog wants the toy that is in your possession and is prepared to perform a particular function for it, how does this differ from holding a piece of food in your hand for the same reason? Either way, the bribery charge still stands—I've got something that you want, do what I ask and you will get it.

The dog's daily food ration is a major highlight of his day. Instinctively food, and the right to eat first and as a result get the richest pickings, will ensure the survival of the best example of the species in the wild state. This driving force is still inherent in the domestic dog and I think it is not unreasonable, when we go to work to earn the money to buy the dog's food, that he should at least do something to earn part of it himself. It is how the food is used that makes the difference between bribery and reward, and Chapters Six and Seven describe some of the ways to do this properly.

But the learning process is not just a matter of giving the dog a reward when he gets it right; sometimes we need to withhold the reward in order to improve the performance.

Before we discuss the mechanics of training, you should realise that we are not simply going to give the dog a tit-bit; there is far more involved than that. When to give it, when not to give it and when to stop training altogether are just as important for you to understand as getting your dog to perform the right behaviour in the first place.

THE TEACHING PROCESS

Some of the exercises that we taught Major would not be necessary for you, if all you wanted was a well-behaved family pet. For example, having established the pack structure which effectively improved his recall and a number of other dominance-related problems, the first formal exercise we taught him was to bark (or speak) on command. This does in fact serve some useful purpose if taught to a pet dog, especially one that is a problem barker, because it puts the barking under the owner's control and this includes the command to stop barking.

By rejecting the Home Office Manual's advice, 'Complete control is the groundwork on which all succeeding training is based', we were able to pick and choose what we taught Major and when, and you can do the same.

It is my experience that the major problems faced by pet dog owners are not coming back when called and pulling on the lead. Generally, as I am sure you are aware, heelwork is the first thing that is taught in a dog club, or the first subject covered in a training book.

Our intention was to test the theory that by increasing Robert's general control over Major in a variety of natural and everyday interactions, and by teaching him some basic obedience manoeuvres, the task of teaching him to walk to heel in a formal manner should not present a problem.

Establishing a clear-cut hierarchical system can effectively overcome many problems. Where they have become particularly resistant, we need to instigate a programme that is designed to eradicate previously learned and naturally self-rewarding behaviour, the most difficult of which is the recall, since before we can train a dog we must be able to catch it.

In Chapter Four I described the difference in Major's attitude as a result of some simple rank restructuring. We were fortunate in that we did not have to work on the problem further, but you might not be so lucky. Refusing to come when called is in itself rewarding to the dog. If you normally find that when you let him off the lead it takes ages before you can catch him again, the chances are that you are going to put him straight back on the lead when you eventually do manage to grab hold of him. The dog obviously learns that coming within catching distance of you results in a loss of freedom for him; not getting caught results in a longer walk with more off-leash fun and games. Your ranting and raving about being late for work only warns him not to come too close to you, and if in the past you have made the mistake of punishing him when you eventually caught him, you can hardly blame the dog for not wanting to get caught in the future. The secret of a good reliable recall is to call your dog, praise and reward him for coming to you and then let him go again. By doing this, you are teaching him that coming to you is a pleasurable thing to do and does not necessarily mean that the walk is over. To be able to teach him this new concept, you obviously have to be able to catch him in the first place. Of course, the standard method of running backwards and drawing your dog in to you at the end of the lead cannot do any harm; it will at least start to show the dog what the word of command means; but on its own, with hardened cases it is not enough.

Let's face it, if the dog is already on the lead there is nowhere else for him to go, and although the majority of people who advocate this method do not suggest that you drag the dog back to you, sadly some do just that. Regardless of the caring attitude of the trainer, some physical influence will then be required, especially if the dog is reluctant to obey.

So how do we overcome long-established and deep-rooted recall problems that do not respond favourably to environmental rank restructuring? Simply by spending a little time changing the dog's expectations about what being called back to you is all about. What follows are some suggestions for you to try.

WHISTLE TRAINING

This is a method which has proved successful in the past and its effectiveness is due to a Russian scientist called Pavlov. He proved that by ringing a bell and then blowing meat powder into the dog's mouth, he could quickly get the dog to salivate when he rang the bell on its own. This is called a conditioned reflex, and what we need to do is to recreate Pavlov's experiment and get the dog to salivate when it hears the tone of a whistle.

Buy yourself a whistle—any whistle will do providing the dog has not heard that tone before. Arrange that part of the dog's daily food ration should be given in the form of tit-bits, so that they can be offered a dozen or so times a day. Whenever you want to give your dog a tit-bit, first blow the whistle, but do not say anything. Do the same when you feed him the remains of the food. After a few days you will notice that the whistle will produce the same results that Pavlov achieved, and you can then start to blow the whistle when your dog is in the garden and you are in the house. By the time he comes through the door, he should be well and truly drooling. Once you have achieved this result, which is no different from the reflex behaviour that we see in our dogs when we pick up their leads or food bowls—purely a reflex reaction to some known and exciting event—you can use it to your advantage: whistle—salivate—return—reward—off you go again.

A variation of this technique can be used on dogs which are not particularly food-orientated and, as with the whistle training, some time should be spent ensuring that you get the proper response from the dog before applying it to the recall. The pre-conditioning process is described below.

KEY WORD TRAINING

For this technique, you need to choose a word or a sound with which the dog is unfamiliar. Just using his name, for example, will not do because he probably hears it a hundred times a day, often when it doesn't even relate to what you want to do with him. 'I need to take Fido to the vet today' or 'I'll go shopping after I've taken Fido for his walk' are examples of how we often use the dog's name without expecting him to respond to it.

If we were observing the dog as we spoke, especially while we were discussing his walk, we would probably see him look up, but because we do not follow it up the dog eventually starts to ignore these sounds. It is in this way that we can start to desensitise the dog towards certain words and what we need to do is exactly the reverse—so that when the dog hears a certain word, even if it is only spoken in a conversational manner, he responds to it instantly. We therefore need to choose a word which is not used in general conversation. If he hears the name 'Fido' many times a day when we don't really want Fido to respond, why not reverse it and say 'Odif' when we do want him to respond?

This new word will now be used to precede anything that the dog perceives as being rewarding to him—a walk, his food, a tit-bit, a game with a toy, in fact anything that happens on a daily basis and which obviously excites the dog. The secret of successfully 'tuning' him in to this word is that you do not in any way telegraph the fact that you are going to use it. Let me explain.

Assume, for example, that you are watching television and decide you are going to take Fido for a walk. Don't get up and have a stretch, then put your shoes on and walk towards where you keep his lead before calling him: these are all signals which tell him that a walk is in the offing, therefore there is no need to call him. Instead, use the key word—'Odif'—and if he does not immediately look at you (which he probably will not the first time) get up out of your chair, pick up his lead and say, 'We were going for a walk, but not if you don't pay attention,' put the lead away and sit down again. By this time Fido will probably be running around the ceiling with excitement, but you should ignore him if possible until he calms down again. Repeat your key word and go through the same procedure until he does look at you the instant you say the word. When this happens, praise him lavishly and take him straight out for his walk.

The same routine should precede all other pleasurable experiences: if he does not pay attention, show him what he would have got if he had.

Within a fairly short space of time, your dog will jump up when he hears the word and come running over to you for whatever reward is to follow. Because no prior clues are being given to indicate what that reward will be, he will be unable to decide whether what he is doing at the time when he hears this key word is more rewarding than what you are offering.

As with the whistle training, remember that key word training starts in the home, not when you are trying to catch your dog in the park with all the other distractions around.

DAILY FOOD RATION

Tit-bits are fine for training most dogs, but usually they are given over and above what is of prime importance to your dog—its daily food ration. In some cases a well-fed dog may find this extra food less of an incentive because he is regularly satiated. With dogs that exhibit problem recalls my APBC colleague John Rogerson uses a technique which takes account of this fact. Briefly, John splits the daily food allowance into ten equal portions, and during the walk the dog gets a tenth of its food for each instant recall. If it does not respond straight away, that portion is put to one side and thrown away when they get home. He estimates that on day one, most dogs only earn about three or four tenths of their usual food ration. On day two, being that extra bit hungry, they probably earn about six or seven tenths. By the end of the week they are earning it all, and he guarantees the success of this method. I have used it myself with particularly resistant recall problems and it certainly does work, providing the owner is prepared not to weaken his resolve that the only way the dog will be fed is by earning its ration.

*   *   *

I have covered recall problems with pet dogs in some depth because in Major's case we had a quick response and therefore little to discuss. These are just some suggestions for overcoming long-established recall problems should the problem still remain after you have firmly established your right to lead your pack. At the risk of labouring the point, this is where the process of all training

MUST start; it then just becomes a matter of overcoming bad habits.

With Major, our task over the next few days was to teach him to bark on command, so that we could test his ability to find hidden people and indicate their presence vocally. We also decided that we would utilise his keenness to follow a ground scent and introduce him to a tracking harness and what tracking was all about.

Searching for a hidden person and tracking are fun exercises for dogs, and by spending the next two or three days play training in these areas, we hoped to develop a working enthusiasm in Major. I realise that they are generally not the sort of exercises that the average pet owner would be interested in teaching his own dog, but if you decide to do so, they will enhance your overall relationship by putting what a dog does naturally under your control, especially when it comes to barking.

We had to teach Major these basic exercises, but the benefits that you will get out of what we did will be from learning *how* we did it. The training principles that follow will apply to anything you want your dog to learn and therefore, regardless of whether or not you want to teach your dog to do the same, they are principles that are important to understand. Personally, I can think of no game that is more fun to teach your dog than to get your children to run off and hide and to be able to send your dog to find them.

6

SPEAK ON COMMAND

The speak (or bark) on command is obviously a very important exercise to teach any dog that will be engaged on police-style duties.

1 As an obedience exercise—to bark when told and to stop barking when told. Anybody who has had anything to do with the training of dogs will tell you that the best way to stop unwanted barking is to put it under command control and then give the 'cease' command when necessary.

2 As a crowd control exercise—to bark *at* a person or a group of people, but only when told to do so, or if a crowd becomes aggressive.

3 For locating hidden, missing or injured people—having found them, to bark at their presence and to remain barking until joined by the handler (great fun as a family/dog involvement).

Some dogs are naturally vociferous, which makes teaching them to bark on command quite easy. Although Major had learnt to bark to seek attention he is not, on the whole, a noisy dog. Before we could start to teach him to look for somebody, we needed to teach him to bark on command. We also wanted to avoid any confusion about what was required and so decided not to use the most common method: waiting for him to bark and then saying 'good boy—speak'. What we wanted was to give the command and get the right response immediately, so that we could reward it. If we waited for him to bark naturally, his attention was likely to be directed towards the object of his barking rather than what we were trying to teach him. We also wanted to avoid confusion about what he had to do to get the reward, so we rejected another tried and tested method—that of telling him to speak and then winding him up with his food or a toy. Although both these methods certainly work, the time from start to successful conclusion takes, with luck, some days; more often than not it takes some weeks.

In general, the dog will be jumping up or lunging forward as it barks, and if it is rewarded for that, then that is what it learns it has to do. If you do not reward the required part of the behaviour (the barking) then it is *never* going to learn what to do. Also, quite often the command 'speak' is repeated many times before the response is achieved, totally against the advice of the Home Office Manual— 'The dog from the first day of training must never be allowed to ignore a command or fail to complete one given'. This, as I have said before, is a principle that I have no wish to dispute. What we wanted, therefore, was that when Robert said, 'Speak,' Major (preferably sitting at the time) would say, 'Woof, woof,' so that Robert could reward him.

We decided to use a behavioural principle called 'successive approximation' or 'instrumental conditioning', both of which sound rather grand but in fact meant that we would reinforce a naturally occurring behaviour which most closely resembled the desired behaviour. Once we had established this, we would put it under command control. To a certain extent this is similar to waiting for the dog to bark at something and then telling him to speak, but that is a hit and miss routine with the command coming after the behaviour and the dog's attention diverted away from the handler. We needed to establish the behaviour, ensure that Major's attention was on Robert and then pre-empt the behaviour with the command.

We simply tied Major to a stable door, took his favourite toy and walked out of lead's length (he was wearing his lead attached to a broad leather collar). No command was given as Robert walked away, and as he turned to face Major he threw the toy in the air and caught it, still without saying anything. Major whined and lunged forward: not what we wanted. He continued to do this for almost a minute and then he lay down: not what we wanted. Robert threw the toy to me and I threw it back. Major sat up, cocked his head on one side and then lunged and barked: not what we wanted. Robert threw the toy in the air again and Major sat down, then he whined and immediately Robert praised him and threw the toy to him. What he had just rewarded was sitting and making a noise (not a bark, just a noise).

It took exactly seven repetitions of this procedure before Major sat and went 'Woof.' The correct behaviour had been established. We had a break lasting about fifteen minutes whilst Major sniffed here and there and Robert and I discussed the learning process of dogs and other animals. Then we repeated the exercise (still with no commands). Major sat immediately and woofed—and was instantly rewarded and released to play. Twenty minutes later we re-created the circumstances, but this time Robert stopped before turning, said, 'Major—speak,' turned and faced him. Major instantly woofed and Robert threw him the toy. We were now putting a guaranteed behaviour under command control. I would stress at this point that Major was not straining on the leash; he was sitting of his own free will and barking for the reward because he had learnt through his own trial and error that this was what worked. After three or four successful repetitions, Robert backed away, stopped and gave the command: instant response. We had now eliminated the secondary visual command of turning.

I would urge anyone who is involved with training dogs, whether your own or others' on a professional basis, to re-read the last paragraph and think about 'what happened'. In a nutshell, this is how dogs learn, and if we cannot grasp this principle, then our ability to train dogs to their maximum will be reduced.

LATENT LEARNING

It was time to call a halt, let Major play for a while and then take him away. This is traditionally called 'stopping on a high note', but in fact there is a behavioural reason for it—it is called *latent learning*, in which information is stored for future use. Students use this technique without realising that they do. They read a poem, for example, just before they go to sleep, and the next morning they are almost word perfect. The trick of latent learning is to try not to learn anything else after the cessation of the exercise. Robert was told to take his dog home, feed him, exercise him on a lead and avoid all unnecessary commands. The next day we set up the same situation in which we had finished before, and the result was that when Robert gave the command 'speak', we got an instant response and Major got instant reward. We now needed to change the criterion for reward from 'woof' or 'woof, woof' to 'woofwoofwoofwoof', and so on. To do this we employed a technique called 'shaping'.

SHAPING

So far, we had rewarded Major for barking without lunging forward, but we had rewarded him for barking only once or twice. What we eventually required was that he would bark on command until he was told to stop barking. To do this, we upped the stakes a little. Instead of rewarding one or two barks, we withheld the reward until we had got three or four. On the first occasion Major 'woofed' and waited: no reward. Then he 'woof-woofed': no reward. Then he lay down: no reward. Then he sat up, lunged forward and 'woofed': no reward. Then he sat, 'woofed', paused, 'woof-woofed', paused, 'woof-woof-woofed'—instant reward. We had now achieved six required responses for one reward; from now on, he would never be rewarded for anything less than six. Twenty minutes later, using the work/play routine, we had shaped his 'speak' to at least ten barks for one command, all of which came without a pause.

Our next step required us to precede the reward with the command 'cease', and Major picked up on this pretty quickly. Within two days of teaching him to bark on command, we had trained the behaviour so that it started on command, continued consistently, and stopped on command—an almost copybook exercise that we now needed to apply to his practical operational work.

Having established that Major would also obey my command to speak for a toy reward, we moved to a different training location, a local farm with areas of woodland. We were going to start to teach Major to search the woods to find where I was hiding, and bark at me until Robert joined us. Naturally, the first step was to get Major to find me and bark, and so having let him see me disappear with his toy, Robert gave the required challenge and then released him to follow me. I had given instructions that Major's reward would be when I threw the toy; I did not want Robert following him or shouting 'good boy' when he did bark. This was to be an exercise between myself (the hidden person) and Major and I wanted all Major's concentration on the job in hand. Too much interference from the handler, no matter how well-intentioned, might distract him.

Major found me without any trouble and was shown his toy held out of his reach. He gave a tentative bark and I praised him as I threw his toy. Two or three repetitions of this resulted in quite a strong and confident bark as soon as he found me. The basics for the 'Search for Missing Persons' exercise had been achieved and Major had loved ever minute of it.

Speak on Finding: Major finds the author and barks for his toy which is being held out of his reach.

Tracking: Major wearing tracking harness, and (below) following a scent trail.

As the weather was kind to us, we concentrated on improving this exercise over the next few days. These games of hide and seek were played in different locations each time and were interspersed with the simple fun tracks that I described earlier (see page 31). As we suspected from our initial assessment of his tracking ability, Major took to this like a duck takes to water. We followed the traditional and accepted methods of training which have to be force free. Following a ground scent, which eventually might be three or four hours old and over a variety of different terrains, requires concentration on the part of the dog. If also requires an expertise that only the dog possesses, so that the handler is entirely in the dog's paws. Therefore, it is obvious that the dog has got to want to follow the scent and you can only encourage a dog to want to do something, you cannot *make* him want to do it. Surely, this should be the basis of all training.

Within four days Major was following a scent trail laid with the wind behind him (no assistance from airborne scent blown towards him), which he had not seen laid although it was still only a few minutes old. The last twenty or thirty yards took a slight deviation to either the left or right, and there was a toy *en route* as well as one at the end to be recovered. He was also enthusiastically searching areas of woodland for me, and on finding me was barking almost instantly without any encouragement. What was also noticeable as the days went by was that when he was thrown his toy he happily and proudly took it to Robert (boding well for the retrieve) and was also walking alongside Robert of his own free will, allowing Robert to go first through gateways without being told to do so—in fact he was clearly more responsive and happy to be led. All this without any formal training as such.

7

BASIC CONTROL

At this stage in Major's training he pulled a muscle in his left foreleg during some off leash exercise on Hampstead Heath where Robert lives. Under normal circumstances, this would have resulted in a rest from formal training until he was sound again. In Major's case, it did not really present a problem. We simply moved the training pro-gramme indoors in order to teach him the basic procedures of the following disciplines:

1   To retrieve properly. This requires the dog to go forward, on command, pick up an article (usually a training dumb-bell) return immediately and sit in front of the handler with the article in his mouth (called the present or offer position).

2   To perform a multiple retrieve. This requires the dog to go forward and perform the same exercise on a selection of previously distributed articles, one after the other. The purpose of this training is to teach the basics of what is known as a property search; the only difference under practical or competition conditions is that he will have to use his nose to detect and retrieve articles that have human scent upon them.

3   Distance control. This requires the dog to stand, sit or down, either on verbal command or by hand signal, without moving forward. Ideally, we would eventually expect Major to go through a combination of these movements, dictated by Robert from a distance, and without Major moving any more than his own body length in any direction.

4   Down with handler out of sight. Eventually, the handler will
    leave his dog in the down position and be out of his sight for
    at least five minutes without the dog moving.

5   Finish to heel. From a sit facing the handler, on the command
    'Heel', the dog goes round from the right and sits by the left
    leg.

Traditionally, all these exercises are taught on the training field
with the dog on the lead, but are we then really *teaching* the dog, or
are we just conditioning it to perform in a particular way? If we
change the conditions, will it still respond in the same way as it would
if it really understood what was required?

The answers to these two questions, even understanding the
meaning behind them, are the key to understanding the difference
between the training techniques that we were employing with Major
and the traditional approach to training.

Let me explain. Take the usual recall training exercise. Whilst still on
the lead, we first teach the dog to stay in the sit position. We walk away
to the full extent of the lead and turn to face the dog. We then command
'Come' and run backwards a few steps, reeling in the slack on the lead.
Any attempt by the dog to go in any other direction is averted by a
gentle pull towards the handler. Once the dog has 'recalled', it is
placed in a sit, in front and facing the handler, and then praised for
coming. One can see immediately that there are far too many elements
to the whole procedure which the dog is expected to learn.

The Sit.
The Stay.
The Come.
The Sit (present), and quite often the dog is also expected to learn to
go round the handler and sit in the heel position.

All this to teach the dog to come when called, and taught in such a
way that the most important element is not really taught but conditioned, because by running backwards with the dog on a lead, the
animal has no other option available to him. To reiterate the advice in
the Home Office Manual:

The dog from the first day of training must never be allowed to ignore a command or fail to complete one given. The dog must never be allowed to suspect that there is even the possibility of being able to avoid a command. It is for this reason that training in all exercises must be commenced when the dog is restrained on the leash and therefore can be instantly guided into the action required. At the commencement of training the word of command may be accompanied by physical influence.

If we take just two of the exercises listed above and look at what is really required from them, we can start to do away with all the formal and in most cases trivial aspects of traditional training. For example, if the dog is taught that the word 'fetch' means 'sit in front of the handler with something in your mouth', it has to go and get the indicated article to do so. Similarly, if it learns that the word 'come' means 'sit in front of the handler in the "present" position', it has to move from wherever it was at the time when it heard the command in order to complete the movement. Simple, really: teach the dog what the word means and it will take the necessary steps to perform the whole exercise.

To teach Major what was required of him from each command, we first allowed him to display a variety of different behaviours in order that he could learn which one would be to his advantage. At the onset, we did not use any words of command; as we had done with the 'Speak' exercise, we rewarded the behaviour which most closely resembled the desired behaviour, established it to an almost guaranteed level, and then put it under command control.

Had it not been for Major's injury, we would probably not have spent so much time 'indoor training', and subsequently we would not have experienced the amazing learning curves that took place during this period. I would add that each session was of just a few minutes' duration with lots of rest periods between them. Taking each exercise in turn, this is how they progressed.

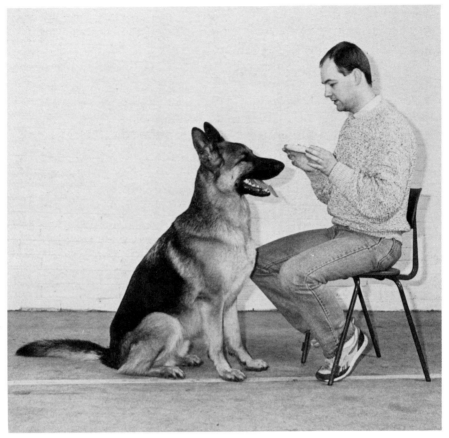

The Retrieve: Initially Major is taught to grasp a piece of piping. Robert holds it out to him . . .

THE RETRIEVE

We had decided that, to begin with, we would not use a dumb-bell; as this would have to be used eventually in the test or for later competition, we did not want anything untoward to happen during the learning process which might cause Major to dislike the article.

We chose instead some hard plastic pipe about twelve inches long and one inch in diameter. The task ahead of us on day one was a relatively easy one—to teach Major that he should sit facing Robert holding the pipe in his mouth. If he could learn that, and then

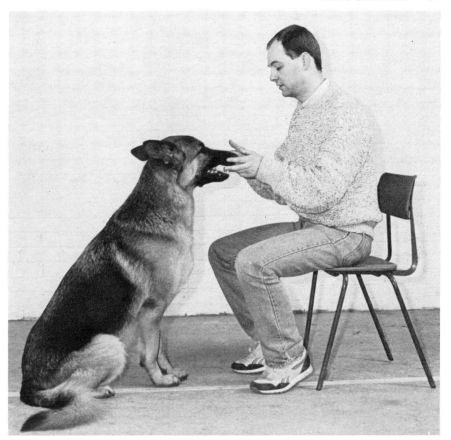

. . . and Major quickly learns to grasp it in order to earn his tit-bit.

associate the same action with the command 'fetch', it would not matter where the pipe was, he would go and get it so that he could sit in front of Robert with it. The same applies to the recall.

We began session one with Robert sitting down on a chair, with Major sitting in front and facing him. Robert showed Major a tit-bit and put it in his pocket. He then showed Major the pipe, which Major sniffed and then tried to root his nose in Robert's pocket. This was ignored and the pipe was offered again, but still Major was intent on getting the tit-bit out of Robert's pocket. This procedure was repeated four or five times and gradually Major lost interest in the tit-bit and

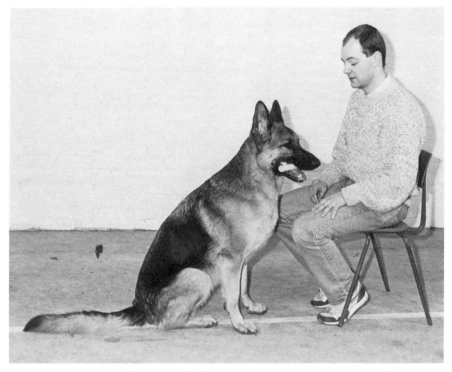

The Retrieve: Major learns to hold the pipe until Robert takes it from him.

started paying more attention to the pipe. Eventually, when Robert offered the pipe, Major grasped it in his mouth, to which Robert responded by immediately producing the tit-bit and rewarding him. The first session ended at this point.

It may be asked why we distracted Major with the tit-bit in the first place. The reason for this was that we wanted to keep his attention on Robert; had we not done so, Major could well have snatched the pipe and run round the room with it. This in itself might have constituted sufficient reward to prompt a repeat performance. Similarly, keeping him on the lead would not have given him freedom of choice, and if his whole attention had been on the pipe a tug-of-war might have ensued, again rewarding him for the wrong behaviour. We wanted him to stay with Robert of his own free will, and to try and find out what he had to do to get the tit-bit.

The Retrieve: After five days, Major fetches the pipe when it is thrown, and returns to present it to Robert.

Some minutes later we repeated the exercise, and Major grasped the pipe in his mouth on the third occasion that it was offered. Within no time at all he was grasping the pipe each time Robert held it out to him; if he did the same the following day, we would introduce the command 'Fetch'.

This is in fact what happened and so, having introduced the command, we now had to teach Major that he should hold on to the pipe until Robert took it off him, not just grasp it and expect a reward. Again, as with the 'speak' exercise, we employed the 'shaping' technique of withholding the reward until a bigger and better performance was displayed (or in this case, longer). What happened next proved to be the first of a number of definite learning curves that were to take place over the following days, one of which was to come from Robert.

The pipe was offered with the command 'Fetch' (we were no longer showing Major the tit-bit first). Major took the pipe, spat it out and looked at Robert's pocket: no reaction. After snuffling the pocket then, interestingly, giving a paw, both of which still produced no results, he picked up the pipe again and looked quizzically at Robert. The fact that he chose to give a paw, something we had not seen him do before, showed that at some point his previous owners had taught him to do this for a reward. Many pet dogs are taught to give a paw or shake hands and most people would say that it is a simple trick to teach them. By the same token, so is the retrieve, because the fact that Major then decided to pick up the pipe as his second choice behaviour proved that he had learnt that this would bring him the desired reward. Whilst he was waiting for a reaction from Robert (hence the look and the obvious learning curve: 'Well, is this what you want me to do?') he was automatically holding the pipe for a longer period. Having counted to five under his breath, Robert took the pipe and gave Major his reward; henceforth he would only ever get rewarded for holding it for this amount of time, until we shaped the exercise for a longer period. Once the process of shaping has begun, the criterion for reward is never reduced.

Still using the work-a-bit, rest-a-bit routine, which was used for all the indoor work, over the next two days we shaped the sit whilst holding the article on the command 'Fetch', and progressed it to Robert standing instead of sitting. On day five, Robert held Major's collar and threw the pipe across the room. Major was given the command 'Fetch', and he did just that. He went out, picked up the pipe and returned, automatically sitting in front of Robert holding the pipe in his mouth.

MULTIPLE RETRIEVE FOR THE SEARCH

At the same time as we were teaching Major to 'fetch' the pipe, we were also going through the same procedure with a variety of other articles—bits of leather, bits of rubber, baling twine, cloth, paper and so on. From an operational point of view, Major might be required to search an area of land at the scene of a crime, and to detect and retrieve any article that had human scent on it. The progression towards day five followed much the same path as did the training with the pipe, except that the upward learning curve for this exercise did not happen until day five.

Having established that he would go forward and retrieve a thrown article, I placed three small articles behind my desk, out of Major's sight. Again holding his collar, Robert threw a fourth article behind the desk and sent Major to 'fetch'. Major went after it and returned to Robert with an article (not the one thrown). He was rewarded and sent back for another, which he instantly did. Both of us were so pleased we naturally expected him to retrieve the third and fourth, but when given the command Major did everything but go near the desk: He barked, he sniffed the bottom of the door, he gave Robert a paw, he sat in front of him, and I could see that Robert was starting to get annoyed.

I was fascinated by the fact that Major obviously realised he should be doing something, but did not know what (forget human concepts; just because he had retrieved two of the objects, it did not mean that he understood what was required, or had the mental agility or logical thought patterns necessary to realise that there were still two to go). What Major did instead was display a variety of learned behaviours. He barked, a recently rewarded behaviour for the speak on command. He sniffed the bottom of the door, an earlier learned house-training technique, probably taught by his previous owners who had trained him to go to the door to be let into the garden. He gave a paw—cute submissive puppy behaviour that had become learned through reward. Sitting in front of Robert was the basis of the exercises that we had recently been teaching. Robert turned to me at this point and said, 'He knows what to do, he's just being bloody-minded.'

Given time, Major would have displayed all his previously learned behaviours, which would have included picking up one of the articles and returning it to Robert. However, human emotions can be very confusing to a dog and the last thing we wanted at this stage was to take a backward step in the rapport that had built up between Robert and Major. We took a 'time out' break—not for Major's benefit, but so that Robert and I could discuss what was happening.

Robert would agree that although he is generally a very sociable person, he does have a short fuse when it comes to inefficiency, whether in his colleagues at work, in the equipment that he is given to use, or in the dog that he has trained. His attitude at this point in the learning curve of the exercise might have permanently affected Major's ability to do the job. This is not meant to be a criticism of Robert as such; I think it is a normal human emotion to express disappointment when what you hope and expect to happen does not. So far, the only punishment that Major had received was the withholding of reward; if I allowed an atmosphere of impatience, exasperation and temper to develop at this point—just when Major was running through his learned repertoire to find the behaviour that would bring some reward—we would be taking a backward step.

To take the view that 'he knows what to do' suggests that Major was making a decision that required an ability to think logically: *I know what you want me to do, but I am not going to do it because you wouldn't give me any of your chips last night.* Humans have this ability, dogs don't. Right from when their senses begin to develop, they learn on a trial and error basis, and the actions that reward them are repeated until they become established behaviour. A litter of puppies at the neonatal stage in their development (0 to 13 days) display totally un-doglike behaviour. During this period their behaviour is experimental; they try to do things that cats do and fail, but when they do things that dogs do they succeed and in this way they eventually start to behave like dogs. At no time during this critical learning period are they punished for un-doglike behaviour, they are just not rewarded for it.

If, using this process, they learn how to behave in a doglike manner at such a young age:

Why have we not taken note of this fact in the past and used it to suit our own training needs in the dog's later life?

They have shown us how easily they can learn; why do we make the whole business so complicated?

Why do we confuse the issue with physical manipulation, physical punishment, complicated training methods and, above all, too much human emotion?

Why can we not accept the fact that a dog is a dog and will never be a human, or display human values?

Why can we not accept the fact that humans learn in exactly the same way? Is it that we have convinced ourselves that there is more to the learning process than lesser animals will ever understand?

The example that I gave to Robert was one that I had heard somewhere in the distant past, the source of which I have forgotten. If he was walking down a street which had litter bins placed at regular intervals and in one of these he saw a £50 note, I would defy him not to look in that same bin every time he passed it. The reward that he had received would ensure that, for a long time, he would always walk on the same side of the street and always glance in the same bin.

As we were talking, Major, who had been lying down next to where Robert was sitting, got up to investigate a noise at the door. Having satisfied himself that it was nothing to worry about, he wandered over to my desk, spotted one of the remaining articles, picked it up and took it to Robert. The look on Robert's face was reward enough for Major, but on my instigation it was still reinforced with a tit-bit. Before Robert could try to encourage Major to fetch the other article, I told him not to say anything. Major looked at Robert for a few seconds as though expecting to be told to do something, then of his own free will he went back to the desk and returned with the fourth article.

My thoughts at the time were, I *think* Major's got the idea; I *know*

Robert has just understood that dogs do not make a conscious effort not to do something: they either do not understand what is required or there is a more rewarding alternative available to them. This was also Robert's personal learning curve.

A little later we set up the same exercise and Major retrieved all four articles without hesitation.

DISTANCE CONTROL

To teach a dog to respond to the down, sit and stand commands is relatively easy if food is used as a lure to get him to perform the right action. As with all exercises, no commands are used until the dog is actually exhibiting the right behaviour.

Sit, Stand and Down

Traditionally, as a quick glance at the majority of dog training books will show you, the dog is put into these positions physically and then praised whilst in the position. I prefer the hands off approach that we used with Major, in which there was nothing to distract him from what we wanted him to learn. In my opinion, if you are exerting pressure on the dog's hindquarters to get him to sit, or pushing down on the withers to get him to lie down (regardless of how gentle this pressure might be), you will automatically create some form of resistance. Not only will the dog resist, it will think about resisting, and if it is doing this it is not thinking about what you are trying to teach it. By eliminating the natural reflex to resist pressure, we automatically made the learning process easier: Major only had to concentrate on what he had to do to earn the reward. Once the movement was established, the frequency of reward was reduced.

THE DOWN. With the dog on one side of a coffee table or similar low obstacle, a tit-bit can be shown and, as the dog goes to take it, gradually withdrawn so that the dog has to lie down to reach it. The instant he does so the tit-bit is given, and eventually the obstacle can be dispensed with.

THE SIT. Offering a tit-bit and, as the dog goes to take it, moving it slowly above and slightly behind the eyeline encourages the head to go up and slightly backwards. Because of the skeletal structure of the dog, this movement can only be achieved if it lowers its rear end. In effect, it has to sit to reach the reward. If your dog insists on walking backwards, use a wall to block the retreat.

THE STAND. From a sitting position, the tit-bit is moved slowly away at the dog's head height. This will automatically draw it forward into a stand, and the reward is given.

These movements were taught to Major on the first day of the indoor training, to the point where he was going from a sit, to a down, back to a sit and into a stand—all for one tit-bit. Although Robert was giving verbal words of command, the way that the food was being used as a lure was also giving Major a secondary visual clue as to what was required. He was learning hand signal commands as well as verbal commands. What we needed to do over the next few days was to get him to do this from a distance.

This proved to be surprisingly simple. We decided that the two major steps to overcome were:

1   If from a distance of six feet Robert raised his hand in the air and said, 'Sit,' would Major respond?

2   If he did respond, would he do it without trying to get closer to Robert?

In fact Major did respond to the verbal and visual commands for sit and down, but when being drawn into the stand, he wanted to keep walking towards Robert. We positioned him alongside the chair in which I was sitting (do you get the impression that we weren't exactly working up a sweat during this training?), clipped his lead on and I held on to it. As he went to walk forward, I held him back—not to check him, but just to stop any further forward progress. Robert then approached him and rewarded him. By day three he was going into the stand position without straining the lead. On day four he was doing distance control without the lead.

The Sit: As Major reaches for the tit-bit, Robert moves it slowly above and behind the dog's eyeline. Major raises his head, and automatically goes into a sitting position, whereupon Robert rewards him.

(Opposite) *The Down: Robert shows Major a tit-bit (top) and, as the dog goes forward to take it, lowers it so that Major has to crawl under the table to reach it (centre). As soon as he lies down (bottom) he gets his reward.*

The Stand: Robert moves the tit-bit slowly away at Major's head height (above), *drawing the dog to his feet to earn his treat* (right).

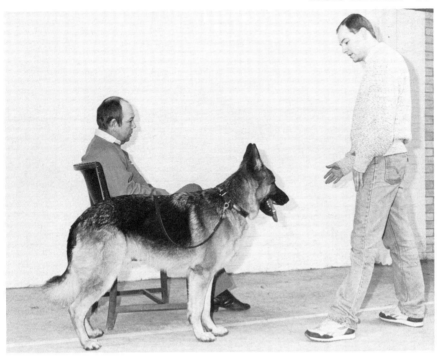

Distance Control: (above) *teaching Major to stand still;* (below) *Down off the lead.*

Distance Control: The Sit (above) *and the Stand, both off the lead.*

This was the only time during the indoor training that the lead was used, but as you will agree, it was not used to force Major to do something, only to stop him doing something. With hindsight, the problem was of our own creation. With the sit and the down, Major was required to perform the action before the reward was given; with the stand, we had encouraged him to come forward towards the hand that held the food. What he was doing by walking towards Robert was exactly what we had inadvertently taught him to do.

When Robert and I discussed this later, we both came to realise that this is another example where, under traditional training methods, we would have been tempted to shout, 'No, stay!' in an angry manner to teach him to stand still. It would eventually have produced the same result, but not without a great deal of confusion for the dog. Our conclusion was that in the past dogs have learnt what to do despite us.

DOWN—HANDLER OUT OF SIGHT

In the past, when I have been judging working trials competitions, it has always been an interesting exercise to look at all the dogs as the handlers walk away from them and try to assess which will stay down for the full ten minutes, and which will gradually creep towards the spot where the handler disappeared out of sight. The dogs that are almost guaranteed to stay look confident and relaxed as they watch their owners walk away; those that are almost guaranteed to fail the test look stressed and anxious.

As a member of the Association of Pet Behaviour Counsellors, I see an awful lot of dogs that vets have referred on to me because they destroy things, soil the house, dig up the carpets and tear the curtains, howl and bark and sometimes self-mutilate when they are left at home on their own. These problems usually come under the heading of 'separation anxiety' and many owners state that they cannot leave the dog, even for two minutes, without the problem arising. In almost every case, the amount of time that the dog is left is not the issue, it is that it cannot be left at all.

The stressed and anxious looks that I see on the faces of the competition dogs that eventually try to rejoin their owners (and invariably get told off for it) show that they are suffering from a similar behaviour problem. In most cases, the handlers will say that in training they try to build up the amount of time the dog is left from one minute to two minutes, five minutes and so on, but in fact they are tackling the wrong problem—they should be working on the dog's attitude to being left full stop, regardless of the length of time.

It is also interesting, and indeed sad, to watch these handlers preparing to leave their dogs. They are very stern, sometimes quite aggressive with their last commands, clearly threatening or daring the dog to get up. This of course increases the anxiety that the dog feels and increases the chance that it *will* get up. They creep back to their owners in a very submissive way and I have heard many a so-called experienced handler comment, 'See, look at him, he knows he's doing wrong.' They then punish the dog for failing the exercise and resolve to do some more training to cure the problem. Unfortunately the training follows the same pattern of *you'd better stay put* and *you bad dog, what did I tell you to do?* A vicious circle is created, with punishment for the wrong behaviour being chosen as the only cure.

I recently spoke to a training society about the normal behaviour of dogs, and during question time somebody raised the subject of a dog that continually failed this part of the test. I explained the similarities between pet dog separation anxiety and the competition dog's view of the whole 'Down out of sight' scenario, going into great depth about the way pet owners usually give their dogs a strict talking-to, or spend a great deal of time reassuring them before they leave—only to punish them upon their return. I was astounded when somebody, who I knew had been 'in dogs' for many years, asked the question, 'But if you don't punish them, how do they know when they've done wrong?' I was heartened when the majority of my audience told him that if the training is done properly, the question should never arise.

I resisted the urge to quote my APBC colleague Peter Neville who, when somebody told him that he had been in dogs for X number of years, replied, 'I have been breathing air as long as that but it doesn't make me a chemist.' The point is that this person had listened to what I had said, but not with his 'middle ear'. The information had entered his head via the organs on each side, but had fallen on stony ground somewhere in the centre, away from real understanding.

How does all this relate to what we were trying to do? Simple! If Major could be taught to stay quietly and confidently in the down position whilst Robert was out of sight for a minute or so, then he would easily accept being left under similar circumstances for a much longer period. I have asked many competitive people who have a problem with their dog in this area, 'Does your dog like to follow you about the house?' They usually reply 'yes' and think that it is a good thing because it shows some measure of rapport and attachment between them. I ask them what would happen if a door got inadvertently shut on the dog. Their reply is frequently that the dog would whine or scratch at the door, and they admit that they normally respond straight away because the dog had not been left in a formal position and they did not intend to shut it out. In fact, what they are admitting is that they cannot leave their dog at all, but they do not relate this basic problem to the difficulty that they are experiencing in their training programme.

Alongside the formal indoor training that Robert and I were doing with Major, I also advised upon the importance of being able to make a cup of coffee in the kitchen whilst Major was shut in the lounge— nothing to do with formal training, just conditioning the dog to being left on his own and realising that it was no big deal.

On day one of the formal training, Major was left in the down position whilst Robert stood in the open doorway. He returned to Major's side, knelt beside him, gently praised him and then rewarded him with a tit-bit. This whole procedure was repeated about four times.

After a break we repeated the exercise, but this time Robert went out of the door and out of sight. Major cocked his head to one side to listen to how far Robert was going, but before he made a decision about whether to follow or not, Robert reappeared and went through the usual praise routine. At this stage we were working on a two-second out of sight; by the end of day one we had extended this period to five seconds.

I was sure that if we could get a comfortable one minute from Major, during which he displayed no stress about being left, then the natural progression towards a full five or ten minutes, or even longer, could be taken in leaps and bounds. By day three of the training,

Major laid his head on his forelegs after about thirty seconds and the minute was completed without any problem. We had no wish to extend the time period just yet, for we had still to conduct the same exercise in other areas, just as we would have to do everything else that had been taught during this enforced indoor period.

FINISH TO HEEL

This exercise is one that puts the polish on other exercises like the recall and the retrieve. Having arrived back at the handler and sat down in a present position, either because he has been called or because he has returned with an article, the dog is required to return smartly to heel. Ideally, he should pass close to the handler's right leg, stay tight to his body as he goes behind him and sit to heel beside his left leg. The quicker and tighter he performs it the more impressive it will look, but at the end of the day it is purely and simply a trick, as is the distance control. It does not require any channelling of natural instincts.

Robert told Major to sit and then stood in front of him in the position that he would be in after a recall or retrieve. Showing Major a tit-bit held in his right hand, he encouraged the dog to follow it round behind his back. He then transferred the food to his left hand and Major was lured into the heel position and rewarded.

As with the other exercises, once we were certain that he would perform the movement, it was preceded with the command 'Heel'. Major is a pretty smart dog, he is also very food-orientated; so it only took two days, using the work-a-bit, rest-a-bit routine, for him to learn this movement.

During this five-day period, Major had learnt the basics of five different exercises and was performing them consistently. Over the next few days and weeks, we needed to ensure that he would perform them in other areas and with other distractions.

At this stage Robert and I reviewed the situation. Major was already fairly proficient in the basics of the following exercises:

Tracking
Searching for hidden person

Play chase and attack
Speak on command
Property/article search
Retrieve
Distance control
Finish to heel
Down out of sight
Recall

But it was whilst we were reviewing his training so far that a couple of other interesting facts emerged. When progressing the distance control from teaching him the movements to getting him to perform them at a distance of six feet, Major had automatically stayed where he had been told whilst Robert walked away. Similarly, when starting the down out of sight, Major had not attempted to move. We had not taught him the 'stay' exercise: we had obviously assumed that he would, and he did. Had he at any time attempted to follow whenever Robert moved, we would have worked on the problem.

As with the recall, we had not had to teach Major to stay because it had come automatically following the rank restructuring. In my opinion, the word 'stay' is surplus to requirements with a trained dog. If the dog has been told to sit, for example, it should remain sitting until told to do something else—go and play, lie down or come here. From a practical point of view, however, it is probably worth teaching the dog what you mean by 'stay' without including it in your formal training for movements like the sit, down or stand. What I mean by this is that if you do not want your dog to follow you, or to jump out of the car when you open the door, teaching him to stay is sensible but does not require him to remain in any particular position—*just don't follow me or move again until I tell you.*

THE STAY COMMAND

The simplest way of teaching the stay is during your rank restructuring programme when it comes to taking control over movement through doorways. In Chapter Four I described the use of Dog Training Discs, and in particular how they are used to ensure that

(Above and opposite) *Finish to Heel: Major sits in front of Robert and is shown a tit-bit in Robert's right hand. Robert moves his hand behind his back and Major follows . . .*

. . . Robert transfers the tit-bit to his left hand and guides Major round to his left side where the dog sits and is rewarded.

your dog grants you freedom of movement in and out of doorways. When using this technique I do not give the dog any commands, for the good reason that I do not want to have to ask his permission to let me to go first. We need to reach a situation where he will step back and allow me to go first out of respect for my higher rank; he can then follow through behind me. Delaying his following will effectively teach him to stay, and this can be done either with the Discs or by simply closing the door on him every time he tries to follow. The procedure would be as follows:

When you approach the doorway, you should expect your dog to take half a pace back to allow you through first—you should not use the stay command to achieve this basic right of rank. Having gone through, your dog will expect to follow you; at this point you tell him to stay, and this command can be reinforced by quickly closing the door on him at the same time (not to trap him in it, just to deny him the opportunity of following you). The routine might require three or four repetitions until the dog does not attempt to follow, and you can then say, 'Good boy, come on, then.' Alternatively, the same principle can be established with the Discs.

Tethering the dog in the car until the routine of 'stay until I tell you to jump out' is learnt can also prove effective. Because the dog is tethered, it physically cannot jump out when you open the door; nevertheless, you still give the command as you open it. Now you are in total control, rather than trying to gain control whilst your dog is trying to get through the first crack of light that appears as the door is opened.

Unclip his lead, but at the same time keep your other hand on the door and repeat the stay command. If he tries to go past you, close the door—again not with the intention of trapping him between the door and the car body since you are not punishing him, just denying him freedom of movement. Three or four repetitions should make him stop and think, and as before, you can then release him. Initially, you should only require him to stay for three or four seconds, but as I said in Chapter Four, dogs often react without thinking about what they are doing. By making them stop, even for just a few seconds, we are making them concentrate on what we are saying instead of just blindly reacting out of habit. Once they are thinking and listening to us, the learning process is almost finished and we just have to show them what we want from them.

Other than from the safety angle of being able to stop your dog from jumping out of the car, or the front door, or the garden gate, the stay command is not required with a trained dog. If it will come to you, and sit or lie down when you tell it, these commands can be used just as effectively for most purposes. If the stay has a use at all, it is to interrupt the dog without asking him to do anything in particular—it is a way of saying, 'Hold on a minute, Fido, concentrate on me for a moment,' and for this reason alone, considering how easily it can be taught, it is well worth the effort.

The other thing we noticed was that when Major was stroked on the withers he no longer shook himself afterwards as he had in the early days of training—a sure sign, in my opinion, that his dominant attitude towards Robert and me was very much reduced. Clearly he was less yobbish in his general attitude, and this was reflected in every aspect of his behaviour. I believed that his automatic 'stay' was a direct result of the environmental dominance training (the natural way to pack leadership) and I hoped that we would see the same results when it came to starting the heelwork exercise. As I mentioned earlier, you can eventually achieve dominance through training, but quite often it is a lengthy process and can be to the detriment of what you are trying to teach. Expressing dominance in a manner that the dog understands, however, will speed up the training programme.

What had been achieved over the first few days of Major's training was a clear-cut understanding that Robert was in charge; Major was also obeying commands which represented the basics of most of the exercises he would eventually be required to do; and at no time had he been reprimanded in a negative fashion.

It will be obvious by now that we had made extensive use of food reward during the indoor training. Whereas my initial introduction to dog training frowned upon this practice—taking the view that dogs should do what you tell them because you have told them, not because you have bribed them—I now have no hesitation in using any means that will encourage the dog to perform the desired behaviour. I reiterate what has been said on a number of occasions: once the behaviour has been established for reward, putting that reward onto a random basis will *always* improve the performance. This is not bribery, it is pure common sense and not dissimilar to the person who works for a wage but improves his or her performance for a bonus.

Channelling the instinctive behaviours of tracking, chasing and searching/barking was done with a toy, but teaching the unnatural/ obedience behaviours needed a greater incentive if Major was going to learn quickly. Whatever the incentive used, as the training progressed, the criterion for reward was pushed to its ultimate limits.

I realise of course that some of the people who read this book will be experienced and very successful handlers and trainers. Of those people I would ask one thing: stop reading for a moment and think about what I have described. It may so far have gone against years of your training indoctrination, but I know it works, and if you can prove that it works for you also, then in some small way we can start to change the face of dog training as it stands in this country today.

8

HEELWORK

One of the things I wished to prove with Major's training was that if control could be established in general, walking to heel would be an almost automatic result. For sure, most dogs get into the habit of pulling on their leads—excitement of the walk, or anticipation of the park are commonly heard excuses for this kind of behaviour.

Correctly assessing your dog, establishing a pecking order, and then teaching him to come, sit, down and so on, will result in a more responsive and respectful dog. Invariably, this makes the teaching of proper leash walking so much easier.

We were both relieved to discover that this in fact proved to be the case. Major was not doing 'Heelwork' as such, but he was not pulling madly on the lead and he was quite attentive towards Robert whenever he changed direction. As with all other exercises, the first formal session of about one minute was completed without any commands being given. Having established the fact that there would be no real pulling problem to correct, we needed only to teach Major that the word 'Heel' meant 'walk from point A to point B at the pace that Robert decides, without sniffing the ground or walking slightly in front, to the side or behind'. To do this, I decided to start with a twenty-yard straight line walk. Major was to be taught on an ordinary broad leather buckle collar attached to a Flexi Leash (not exactly the macho Police Dog piece of training equipment, but a device which I have found invaluable in overcoming the learned pulling and constant sniffing habits of pet dogs).

To understand how a Flexi Leash can be used to teach heelwork, we first of all need to examine the whole business of teaching this exercise, and to understand why the majority of dogs continually pull on the lead, despite the fact that many pet owners attend training classes to teach them not to. In class, they will eventually become very good; outside class they revert to imitating Huskies in a sled race.

It is a well-known scientific fact that pressure invites equal pressure. I have made this statement many times in my two previous books; I have also explained it in some depth in the correspondence course 'The Canine/ Human Interface', that I wrote and tutor for the Canine Studies Institute (Ascot House, High Street, Ascot, Berks, SL5 7JG).

To demonstrate how this fact of life affects the dog's pulling activities, stand with your dog on a lead, very gently pull the lead towards you and watch your dog start to lean in the opposite direction. I realise that the correct use of the lead is to give a swift check and release, but the average pet owner does not have the skill and the timing to do this properly; the inevitable result is that he or she pulls one way whilst the dog pulls the other.

To teach heelwork using the traditional method, the Home Office Manual tells us: 'the dog should be given every opportunity to make mistakes and if caused mild discomfort when out of position, but praised by voice and hand when correct, it will soon learn the correct position it should occupy.' I have seen how some handlers cause 'mild discomfort' and anyway, to suggest that this is a standard training technique does not take into account each dog's individual touch sensitivity: what is mild to one dog may be very severe to another.

We know what we are trying to teach by using this method—being alongside us is nice, not being alongside us is unpleasant—but I believe we should think carefully about what the dog *might* be learning. It hears the word 'Heel' and the handler starts walking. As an untrained dog, it forges ahead and experiences some 'mild discomfort' (lovely phrase). Whatever happens after that is of no consequence: what we are effectively doing right at the start of the teaching process is linking physical discomfort with a word of command. Of course, given time the dog will learn, as dogs have done for decades, but it is my submission that we are placing obstacles in the path of easy learning.

Most people would accept that very few dogs learn to walk to heel on a lead in just one training session: it takes many repetitions before the dog understands what is expected when it hears the word 'heel'. Again I submit that the reason for this is that the technique actually confuses some dogs.

It should be understood that if a reaction occurs following a dog's action it will learn from the experience. The action must occur *within two seconds* if the dog is going to learn quickly. If the reaction to its action is rewarding, this increases the possibility that it will repeat the action. If it is unpleasant, it increases the possibility that the dog will not repeat the action. Bearing this in mind, what are we teaching a dog when we use the procedure of 'Heel', check, 'Good dog'? We *may* teach the dog that walking in front is unpleasant; we *will* teach the dog that the word 'heel' is a negative word and a prelude to punishment. For sure, in time we can teach it that there is a pleasant alternative, but what a long drawn-out, confusing business it is.

Using a Flexi Leash with the brake released (I use a Flexi 8), there are twenty-six feet of leash available to the dog before there is any pressure to resist.

Problem one has been overcome: If you don't pull backwards, the dog cannot pull forwards.

All it can do is walk faster than you, but if as it goes forward you swish the handle in a downward arc and at the same time lightly apply the brake, you can create a rapid 'click click click' noise that captures the dog's attention. Because this noise is being produced by the brake rubbing across the ratchet inside the handle, it causes the end of the lead, which is attached to the dog's collar, to judder. In turn, this juddering interrupts the dog's natural movement and causes its front legs to do a little dance.

Problem two has been overcome: it is impossible to walk faster.

In our case, problem three had already been overcome by establishing the rank structure between Robert and Major, so there was already an in-built instinct that Robert should set the pace and direction.

Problem four (that of confusion over the command) never arose, because until Major learned the futility of trying to walk faster than Robert, no commands were given. The only words that were spoken during the first minute or so were when Major slowed his pace to Robert's and looked up at him as a natural reaction to the noise that was coming from above and behind. Robert smiled and said, 'Good boy.'

Within two minutes Major was walking to heel, whether the pace was slow, normal or fast. YES, TWO MINUTES! We could therefore start to increase the reward for walking alongside Robert. It should be obvious by now that having taught Major, without saying anything, that it was impossible to walk in front, we could henceforth ensure that only pleasant experiences were associated with the command 'Heel'.

Heelwork: The clicking of the Flexi Leash brake and the judder keep Major from forging ahead, without need for a word of command.

We decided to reward Major with a play article at the end of each 'heelwork' session, for two main reasons. Firstly, because we had already started to put tit-bit reward onto a random basis—he was now only being rewarded with food for the biggest, fastest and best response—and therefore food reward for heelwork would be very occasional and would serve as a jackpot bonus. Secondly, because we needed to make Major very 'article conscious' to increase his enthusiasm in the exercises for tracking and searching for lost or stolen property. This meant that anything—whether of string, rubber, wood or metal—would be a potential play article between Major and Robert and therefore worth picking up or competing for. Many of the top handlers in this country have a particular 'happy article' for their dogs, which the dog associates with play and which is used for a reward at the end of a training session. It is interesting to note that a lot of handlers who use this technique will still frown on the use of food for training, but have yet to explain to me what the difference is—surely an incentive is an incentive.

I have also found that where a particular 'play toy' is used, some dogs become fixated on it. They will track like a dream, but ignore all the articles except that particular one. They will search an area and clearly indicate the presence of something with human scent upon it, but will then ignore it and continue their search. They are looking for their play toy. My APBC colleague John Rogerson uses this toy fixation to overcome behaviour problems in dogs. In effect, what he does is to centre the dog's whole world around a particular toy—it works like magic if the correct preconditioning programme is followed, and as a result of what I have learnt from John I often use it myself. However, it can have a reverse effect on a working dog, just as the use of food can do if it is not used properly: you may create a situation where the dog will only work for this particular reward.

The next stage with Major, therefore, was to give the command 'Heel' and walk twenty or thirty paces in a straight line (smiling and giving the occasional 'good boy'); if the Flexi Leash was needed to regain his attention, no commands were given, just verbal and visual praise for being in the right position. After the chosen distance, Robert would take a pace backwards, give his release from working signal, 'Off you go', and throw an article for Major to chase. Each

A patrol leash is introduced, but not as a training aid.

Within two days Major is walking to heel without the lead, and clearly enjoying it.

time, it was a different article. Although some turns to the left or right were introduced later on in the session, no halts were included for sit, stand or down positions. Towards the end of the second day Major was walking to heel without the lead, and not because we were rushing things: it was obvious that he was ready to do so. Both Robert and I were amazed at the rapid progress the dog was making and we were becoming more and more convinced that we were on the right road towards compulsion-free training.

Our next task was to teach heelwork which included the sit, stand and down, and at the commencement we reverted to the Flexi Leash. The only exercise which created any problem was the stand.

Whenever Robert stopped Major wanted to sit, and although this was solved very simply by anticipating the sit and slightly touching the inside of the stifle with his left hand, it took a number of repetitions before it suddenly dawned upon me why the confusion was arising. Whenever I said to Robert, 'OK, let's do some more heelwork,' Robert would call Major to heel, stand very straight in the traditional heelwork stance and tell Major to sit.

All of us tend to do the same thing: whenever we decide to carry out any formal training we adopt this 'training attitude'. On reflection, what I cannot understand is why, whenever we decide to do anything, we always start with the word 'sit'.

Let's do heelwork!
OK. *Sit*.
Let's do a retrieve!
OK. *Sit*.
Let's do a search!
OK. *Sit*.

The list can go on and on, and we probably do it because it is the easiest position from which to get the dog to perform, in order that the training upon which we are about to embark starts from a controlled situation. It is also probably the first thing that any puppy owner teaches a dog to do and I have noticed over the years that whenever a dog becomes confused about anything, it sits. In other words, it reverts to a situation that has rewarded it in the past—the sit becomes a conditioned reflex. We therefore decided to start each heelwork session from the stand and—bingo!—Major understood.

Over the next few days we progressed from halting in the sit, down or stand, through halting and then leaving Major in any one of these positions (a fairly simple leave and return procedure) to stopping him in a position whilst Robert continued to walk on. In obedience circles, this is called 'positions on the move'.

Again we reverted to the Flexi Leash, but this time I held it and walked behind them both. Once Major overcame his curiosity about being followed, we were able to teach him this advanced heelwork routine, first at the slow pace. If Major tried to follow, I would simply apply and release the brake and leave it to Robert to return gently and re-position him. It only took four or five repetitions before we had reached the stage where my mechanical influence was no longer needed.

I stress the fact that Robert returned to Major *gently*, and by this I mean that all he did was turn round and walk back to him without even looking directly at him, get him to adopt whatever position he should have been in and walk away again—no fuss or emotional displays, no reprimand for getting it wrong, no praise given until he was able to return to Major whilst he was still in the right position.

Working with Robert and Major over these weeks enabled me to put a lot of my theories into practice. Without doubt, both of them responded well to the techniques employed, and for this I have to give a lot of credit to Robert. He was not a novice handler, as I have previously stated; indeed his previous experience was the one factor that I thought might cause some difficulty in introducing a new concept, because in the past he had successfully worked dogs which had been trained with the traditional praise and punishment techniques.

His comment, when we discussed the effect of changes in handler attitude, was that, had we not started to get results so quickly and so calmly, he would not have been so receptive to a different (non-punitive) approach.

As part of the training programme, I arranged that Robert should 'sit in' and listen to some of the problem behaviour cases which had been referred on to me. I felt quite strongly that if he was really to understand his dog, he should hear about some of the 'pickles' that the average pet owner gets into with his or her dog and why.

We were extremely lucky, at the time when we were trying to teach Major 'positions on the move', to see a dog which had become aggressive towards people, but was more than just a pet. This dog had been trained for obedience competition and had qualified to a very high standard. To cut a long story short, the dog's change in behaviour proved to be diet-related (an area which is outside the scope of this book, but discussed in greater detail in my other books). Having sorted out the pressing problem, we then got on to discussing training problems, simply because, in conversation, my client found out that I had formerly competed with my own dogs. It transpired that the biggest problem was the 'stand' on the move. Both Robert and I exchanged a glance, which I hope my client did not see. We took the dog out to the training area and commenced some competition heelwork.

When the dog was given the signal to 'stand', whilst the handler kept walking, he did stop momentarily, then his ears went back and his head went low and he started to creep forward. The handler, who was watching over her shoulder to anticipate the movement, turned immediately and shouted, 'NO! STAND!' The dog slunk into a very submissive down position which brought the handler rushing back to reprimand the dog and reposition him in a stand.

Clearly the dog was worried about the whole affair and, equally clearly, the handler's 'over the shoulder' look was read as a prelude to being told off, which was why he was trying to follow in a submissive manner and why he showed even more submission the moment he was shouted at for following. Obviously, he understood the word 'stand', which was why he stopped instantly and, providing the handler was quite close, he had no problem. The problem only arose when the handler moved farther away, and she was increasing his insecurity by (understandably) watching to see what he was doing.

As I have stated before, dogs do not deliberately do things wrong; to do so requires a logical thought process. Punishing them for it does not necessarily teach them to do it right, but what it can do is teach them to dislike the exercise. We discussed the methods and the theories behind Major's training for this exercise, and Robert demonstrated the results. Her comment on watching as Robert returned was that Major's tail started to wag the moment Robert turned round. The difference between the two dogs was that Major was *expecting reward*, her dog was *expecting to be told off*.

Overcoming her problem was not going to happen overnight. Before the dog started to learn what to do, it had to learn not to be fearful of her when she left it in the stand position. I was pleased to hear later that, with the help of a friend, she did overcome her problem, and one or two others for that matter, by using the same positive approach that we were using with Major.

This particular problem, coming at the time when we were teaching Major the same routine, helped by providing a classic example of the different results obtained through the two schools of thought.

9

HOW NOT TO TRAIN YOUR DOG

At this point I would like to digress from Major's training in order to discuss in more detail some of the problem side-effects that can be caused through using punishment during training, as a way of teaching the dog that it has just done something wrong. The case described in the last chapter, where the dog was told off for not standing still, is a classic example of how, if negative methods are used, the problem can get worse.

As I have explained, all my clients are referred to me by their veterinary surgeon because their dogs are exhibiting some behaviour problem or other. I no longer 'train' dogs as such, except for my contract with the City of London. It is a fact that dogs which have been trained for a specific task and are regularly involved fulfilling that task, either working or competing, rarely exhibit behaviour problems. Occasionally they do, as the last example proved. It is unusual, therefore, for me to see clients whose dogs are involved with their work or their hobby. When I do, and they find out that I have worked dogs and competed with them myself, at the end of the consultation they usually ask my advice about one of their own training problems.

A recent example of this was a dog who 'crabbed' during heelwork. Crabbing is where the dog is constantly impeding the handler's ability to walk properly because it is too far forward and turned inwards across the handler's left leg. This handler was a big, strong man and his dog, a Dobermann, was just as macho-looking. The behaviour problem was that he had become aggressive towards the man's wife and children. Briefly, because this book is not about behaviour problems, the handler was a very strict disciplinarian with his dog and would not tolerate the slightest infringement of his rules. The result was that his dog was constantly being physically punished at home and in training. I myself would not have liked being physically punished by him—he was big!

His family had adopted the same attitude towards the dog, and whereas the dog was prepared to accept punishment from the man, he was not going to tolerate the rest of the family taking the same liberties. In fact, the problem was a classic example of what I said in Chapter Two—that a lower rank should not tell a higher rank what to do. If the man told the dog to lie down and he did not instantly obey, he was forcibly pushed to the ground. (Remember the Home Office Manual: 'The dog from the first day of training must never be allowed to ignore a command or fail to complete one given . . . At the commencement of training the word of command may be accompanied by physical influence'.) This man worked on the commonly held training principle that if you have told a dog to do something, it must obey, and he had instructed his family to follow suit.

The problem was that the dog saw himself as number two in the pecking order—in fact the man treated the dog as the next highest ranking, because it accompanied him everywhere. He worked nights and took the dog with him. During the day the dog slept in his bedroom and on his nights off, when the man slept with his wife, the dog growled at her when she entered the bedroom. This resulted in him getting a thump from the man and being banished to the kitchen. If the kids told the dog to 'sit' or 'down', the dog would growl at them, too, basically because he was defending himself against the possibility that they might start pushing him around. This resulted in another thump from the man and again being shut out. In canine terms, this dog was very confused. He could not understand why, when he was disciplining lower ranks for what he saw as an infringement of the pack rules, he was attacked by the pack leader. Rather than teaching him not to do it, which was the obvious intention, the punishment was building up resentment and increasing the dog's aggression. Contrary to how this might sound, the handler was not a cruel man—in fact, once he had overcome his years of indoctrinated beliefs and started to view things from his dog's point of view, he was horrified at what he had done. It came as quite a shock to him to discover that the problem was his fault, which was the last thing he expected to hear—after all, he was the only person who did not have a problem with the dog.

I have briefly explained the circumstances that led up to his visit because, after I had spent two hours getting him to really understand his dog and how to restructure the pecking order on a non-confrontational basis, he became more open-minded and willing to try an alternative approach. He freely admitted that he had been very sceptical about coming to see me, but his vet had basically given him two choices—see me, or put the dog down. With his many years of training experience (this was not his first dog), in his own words he did not believe in 'all this psychological clap-trap'. Apparently, what had given me some credibility was when he found out 'that I had actually got my fingernails dirty with dogs'.

Having heard how strict he was with the dog, I already suspected what the problem was with his heelwork, but I needed to see him work his dog to confirm my suspicion. Sure enough, as soon as he adopted his 'training' stance, the dog became very tense. As soon as he started to walk, the dog started 'crabbing'; his ears were tight back on his head, which automatically gives the Dobermann a very wide-eyed appearance—this was not a happy dog. He was of course wearing the obligatory choke chain and I had already been repri-manded for calling it this in my office: 'It's not a choke chain, it's a check chain'. Tell that to the long-necked, thin-coated, generally touch-sensitive Dobermann and see whether calling it something kinder reduces its effect: this dog was not happy wearing it. I asked him to do an about-turn and was not surprised to see the typical 'spin on the spot' turn of an obedience competitor. I had seen enough and told him to let his dog run off and play whilst we had a chat.

His first question was how I could tell what the problem was when he had only walked ten paces and done one about-turn. My answer was that I had just watched the dog's reaction. In answer to my question about what had he done to try and cure the problem in the past, I was told that his instructor had suggested that he step on the dog's toes. When this did not work, they had fitted the dog with a pinch collar which, as you can see from the photograph overleaf, looks like something which the Spanish Inquisitors would have used to train their dogs.

Someone had suggested doing only left-hand turns, which was actually sound advice, but he had not persevered with this because he felt that it was avoiding the problem and not curing it as the other two techniques were designed to do.

I do not even wish to comment on the stupid advice to tread on the dog's toes, but I will comment on the use of the pinch collar, sometimes called a prong collar and often, incorrectly, a spiked collar. Although I would never use one myself and am totally opposed to them, to be fair, I have seen one of these used by an expert on a very touch-insensitive pulling dog with good results. The dog responded very quickly with only the slightest bit of pressure being exerted by the demonstrator and with no stressful side-effects being shown by the dog. My fears as I watched this demonstration are becoming reality, however, for this piece of equipment is becoming more widely available and very much misused. To use one on a touch-sensitive dog is nothing short of cruelty and no different from

The pinch collar.

stomping on its feet. Every piece of training equipment has its use, on the right dog, used in the right way, by the right person, for the right reason. Unfortunately, people see impressive demonstrations by experts, obtain the equipment and then use it willy nilly to try and impress other people, usually at the expense of the poor dog. The method used to teach Major to walk to heel works with most dogs, regardless of their touch sensitivity.

In this case, both the handler and his instructor were approaching the problem from the 'how can we cure it?' angle, and using punishment/pain to try and achieve this. What they should have been asking was, 'Why is the dog doing it?' Had they done so, they would have found the answer.

The chain hurt—this was evident from the stressful expression that the dog adopted as soon as the handler took up his training attitude. A very slight squeeze of the webbing between the dog's toes proved just how touch-sensitive he was. In fact, this dog would have been responsive to a piece of cotton around his neck; he certainly did not need the rigours of a choke chain, and even less a series of prongs squeezing into his neck.

Using a demonstration technique which I was shown many years ago by a very forward-thinking trainer called Roy Hunter, I asked the man to act as if he were my dog whilst we did some heelwork. We set off and he walked alongside me. Without any warning, I suddenly spun round and set off in the opposite direction—which was what he had done when I had told him to about-turn. Within a fraction of a second there was a gap of three or four feet between us, with him in what would be termed a lagging position. Had he had a chain around his neck, attached to a short lead, it would have tightened without any influence being applied by me. Had I adopted the same 'instant obedience is paramount' attitude, as was his towards his dog, I would have given the lead and chain a quick yank and growled 'Heel'.

To give the guy his due, he understood the problem instantly. His eyes rolled towards the heavens as he reached what I call the 'AH-HA' level—'AH-HA! so that's why he "crabs". I spin round, which effectively puts him into a lagging position; I punish him for something which I have caused, he tries to compensate by anticipating my about-turn; I then try to cure it by punishing him further.' Within about five minutes of doing some gentle heelwork with the dog on a broad leather collar, giving him a command before the about-turn and slowing down the turn to give the dog a chance to keep up, we had produced a remarkable improvement in the dog's attitude: he became more relaxed and already did not 'crab' as much.

As with the case in the last chapter, the cure will not happen overnight; there will be many months of suspicion to overcome on the dog's part, about what might happen next. Dogs are remarkably resilient creatures, though; they forgive us very easily providing we eventually start to treat them properly. Perhaps this is why we abuse them so much under the banner of training. I am sure my wife would say that I have many character faults, most of which I would of course deny. But one to which I would freely own up is the smug feeling that I get when I can turn someone's world upside-down after they have arrived at my premises with the 'might is right' attitude.

In this particular case, my client's problems—the dog's aggression towards his family—were inadvertently his fault, and his training problem was also his fault because he had been ill-advised. In fact, all his problems stemmed from the fact that he wanted a well-behaved dog at home, as well as a successful dog for his hobby of dog obedience competitions. Considering the fact that, deep down, this big, strong man's intentions were right, feeling smug is perhaps not the right phrase—a terrific sense of achievement and success would be better. Ho hum: a rose by any other name!

*   *   *

The following story dates from a time some years ago, when I was still helping people with their training difficulties but was becoming increasingly aware of the need to sort out the behavioural aspects first. Indeed, I initially heard about the problem from someone who had previously seen the dog and had advised a dominance reduction programme, but felt that some extra training would not go amiss. Although it shows that, sometimes, a misdiagnosed behavioural approach can also exacerbate a problem, I have included the story to show that whether you are deciding upon a behavioural or a training cure, you must first of all *understand* the cause.

I received a phone call from a woman in Reading, who was concerned about her GSD's behaviour towards people and in particular towards her 19-year-old son. As I have explained, she had previously sought advice and had been told that the dog should be demoted within the household, and that the status of her son should be raised. The dog in question was a two-year-old male, and the household consisted of the female owner and her elderly mother, with whom he lived for five days a week. At weekends and holiday times, the son came home from college.

The situation had deteriorated to the point where the dog was defending its house and immediate territory against all intruders, and when the son returned it showed aggression towards him every time he told it to do anything. Based upon what I had already been told about the advice that had been given, and considering the circumstances, I also naturally assumed that we were talking about a dominant dog that was resenting the challenge of the only other male member of the household, who was not there on a permanent basis.

When I arrived at the house I was shown into the living-room and the dog, although obviously slightly agitated about my presence, accepted the fact that I had been allowed in and settled down in the corner of the room, keeping a wary eye on me—and I on him. All the members of the household were present and they started to relate to me some of the circumstances in which the dog showed aggression toward the son. These only confirmed in my mind that we were dealing with a dominance problem. After about twenty minutes the elderly lady served us all with tea and biscuits, and at this point the dog left the corner of the room and came and positioned himself alongside me, obviously recognising a soft touch when he saw one. Having obtained the owner's permission, I offered the dog a biscuit, telling him to SIT. This command was met with a deep-throated, lips-back snarl, to which the son responded by jumping up and shouting, 'See! That's what he does to me, now you've seen what he's like.' What I noticed was that instead of his tail being erect when he growled, it was kept down and the tip of it was wagging slightly. What I was seeing was not dominance aggression, it was fear.

It should be noted at this point that all dogs can snarl/growl; similarly, they can bark and bite—it's what dogs do. In a snarl/growl which indicates an intention to attack, the mouth is funnelled forward and the rest of the body takes on a forward appearance, which usually includes a high tail carriage. A snarl/growl which indicates an intention to defend if necessary would normally show a more wrinkled nose and backwardly drawn lips, effectively showing more teeth. The rest of the body would also take on a retreating posture in lots of subtle little ways, including the tail carriage.

The dog's aggressive display led me to follow a different line of questioning, and we started to trace the dog's previous training and learning experiences in more depth. It transpired that whilst he was still quite young (eight months) they had attended a dog club which the dog, after the first two or three sessions, clearly did not like. He started to panic at the door of the club, but the son was told that he should not allow the dog to behave in such a way and that he must be made to go through the door. This went on for two or three more sessions until the son decided not to take him any more.

They decided to enlist the help of a private trainer who came round to the house and started to teach the dog in the back garden. During the first lesson, whilst engaged upon his first formal heelwork exercise, the dog started to fool about, which with hindsight was probably a sign of stress. Unfortunately, this was rewarded with a severe yank on the choke chain, whereupon the dog growled and was immediately lifted off the ground and swung round at the end of the lead before being crashed back to earth on his side. The trainer instructed the son to react in exactly the same way, each time the dog showed any signs of aggression. To cut a long story short, what this dog had learnt, from this and his previous dog club experiences, was that any command was a prelude to a physical confrontation and, being a dog that was basically lacking in confidence, the aggression he was showing was a form of defence.

There was obviously an element of male rivalry involved, which was also contributing to the unacceptable behaviour, but the early training experience was the root cause. By changing all the commands and using a system of training based upon positive reinforcement, we were able to overcome the dog's suspicion of commands and what might follow, although we shall never be able to overcome completely the dog's very natural suspicion of humans and their unpredictable behaviour. Understanding the root cause at least allowed the owners to recognise the fact that they had triggered off a fear reaction in their dog, so that they did not automatically take the normal human approach that *'no dog's gonna growl at me'*.

It is extremely hard for us to grasp that, when a dog starts to growl at us, it may be WE who are at fault. It is even harder for us to grasp that we can stop the growling by relieving the pressure which we may be putting on the dog at the time; we automatically regard this as rewarding the behaviour and letting the dog win. But at the end of the day, we pride ourselves on being a highly intelligent species, and if WE reach a situation where we are prepared to use aggression to defend ourselves and then find we do not have to carry out the threat—are we not relieved? As a highly intelligent animal, can we not recognise the same defensive attitude in another species?

In this particular case, the owners are at least now able to understand and control their dog, whereas before, euthanasia was being considered as the only alternative.

At the risk of becoming boring, it can clearly be seen that the dog had a very good reason for showing aggression, and it should also be quite obvious that any training approach which involves punishment for wrong behaviour, which caused the problem in the first place, would only compound that problem in the future.

I would not want the reader to get the impression that, by quoting these examples, I am suggesting that this is normal treatment by trainers and clubs—it is not. As I have already stated, there is a growing army of more enlightened people who are dedicated to improving and advancing dog training techniques. They rightly work on the principle that, rather than tell a dog what it has done wrong, you should tell it what to do right instead. Confusion between what we are trying to teach and what the dog is actually learning lies at the heart of many problems. I have just received a telephone call from a woman who is having difficulty house-training her young dog. She taught it to go on paper in the kitchen, praising it every time it did so. She gradually moved the paper to the door and, when it started going to the door, she took the paper away and let it out into the garden. She now lets it out regularly.

This is a standard approach which works with most dogs. The

problem in this case is that the dog goes into the garden and plays (that's all). When it comes back into the kitchen, it relieves itself and gets told off for it. The situation now is that it still relieves itself in the kitchen, but only when she is out of the room.

When she thought she was teaching her dog to use the paper and gradually moving it towards the door so that the dog would give her some indication that it needed to go, the dog was learning that it got praised for going in the kitchen. When it continued to go in the kitchen and started to get told off for it, the dog became confused about the whole business except for one thing: don't go in front of mum, she's got some sort of weird hang-up about it.

The answer to the problem was simple. Stop the punishment, he is not doing it to spite you. Retrain the dog in such a way that it understands exactly what it should be doing. Contain it in its sleeping area when it is not supervised (dogs do not like to soil their nests). At the guaranteed times and frequently in between, take it from its nest to a specific area in the garden and wait until it performs. Reward it, not just with praise, but with a juicy tit-bit or favourite toy to which it only gets limited access after the desired act. It can then have supervised freedom back in the house; when unsupervised it must go back to its bed.

This technique (called target training) takes just a few days to learn. It avoids confusion and negates the use of punishment for the wrong act. It might involve some extra effort on behalf of the owner, but if we are not prepared to teach our dogs what we want them to do, we should not have a dog in the first place.

If we have reached a situation where we are considering ways of punishing our dog's wrong behaviour, we should stop and think about why it has not learnt the right behaviour. Invariably, re-teaching by using an error-free training method will overcome the problem.

This is what Major's training was all about: we were not telling him off for doing it wrong, we were only rewarding him for doing it right. For sure, he might at some point do what we did not want him to do and, in some way beyond our control, get rewarded for it. This was something of which we would have to be aware as we progressed his training from the basic concept to the finished product, but, as you will see in the following chapter, we could ensure that this would happen without spoiling the relationship between dog and handler. The purpose of the present chapter has been to show how NOT to train a dog and to make you aware that there are still people around who will tell you adamantly that you can only train a dog through physical domination and by punishing unwanted actions.

10

PROGRESS—ADVANCING THE TRAINING

Let us return to Robert and Major. We had now taught Major to walk to heel and stop in any given position (stand, sit or down); stand, sit or down at a distance; retrieve; search and retrieve articles containing human scent; stay down whilst the handler was out of sight; recall on command and finish to heel; speak on command; search and indicate the presence of someone hidden; and track a person by ground scent alone. As far as I was concerned, he was more highly trained after six weeks than the average pet dog would ever be required to be. All this without any negative circumstances and having spent only a few minutes a day on any one exercise. At the same time we had been working on the basics of his criminal work exercises which, as I previously stated, I shall not describe in detail, since the object of this book is to help people to understand how to train their own pet dogs just to be better companions.

At the end of six weeks Major was reasonably proficient in everything that was required of him except the agility which, considering his age and size, I had no intention of introducing until it was absolutely necessary. Teaching big young dogs to jump can place tremendous stresses on their still-developing joints and bone structure and many a good young dog has been ruined, or its working life shortened, through being made to jump too high, too young. Before the course started, I had made it clear that he would only be asked to show his ability to jump under control, and this had been agreed.

We had been given the benefit of a twelve-week course. I was already content that my experiment had proved successful, except for the final assessment (he needed to achieve 70 per cent of the possible overall marks). We therefore had a further six weeks to put the icing on the cake and go for maximum marks. What he actually scored and what happened during his assessment will be recorded in Chapter Twelve. This chapter is about the six-week bonus period, during which some interesting things happened—the most noticeable being that when we began to progress some of the exercises, we unexpectedly ran into difficulties. And when things started to go slightly wrong I had a lot of soul-searching to do.

It was my responsibility to train Robert and Major to a laid-down standard, within a period of time that has been proven to be adequate, using traditional methods.

Robert had been an excellent student because he had seen the early results and trusted my judgement, but at the end of the day he expected to be allowed to resume operational duties with a qualified dog.

When, for example, Major started to spit out the retrieve object before sitting in front of Robert, or refused to stand during distance control (things which he had previously shown he was perfectly capable of doing) I began to wonder whether an element of *'me man, you dog—I say, you do!'* should be included as an essential ingredient.

In short, I began to consider ways of punishing the wrong behaviour, which was perhaps a reflection of my early indoctrination into dog training—or perhaps just a reflection of a typical human attitude towards dogs. If the latter was the case, at least it showed that I was human. In the end, we did not need to resort to compulsion, but only because I was reluctant to do so and needed time to think about it. We decided to leave the problem for a few days.

THE PROCESS OF LEARNING

In Chapter Six I mentioned the beneficial effects of *latent learning*. As I understand it, latent learning works when you finish something on a high note, or complete something successfully and then rest, or at least stop. Basically, the last behaviour completed is the one that is remembered. If the behaviour was good (from the subject's point of view) the next will be as good or better. If it was bad, the next will be as bad or worse. Every dog trainer worth his or her salt will tell you always to finish a training session on a high note, but do they know why? The general opinion (and I have researched this) is that the dog will finish with happy memories of the session and so be keen to train again. This is actually wrong: all that happens is that the last exercise will be improved, usually the one exercise which does not need improving.

When the brain shuts down from an active state to a restful or sleeping state, it transmits different waves. Memories of what has happened during active brain function can transfer to the dormant brain function—it's why our dreams may sometimes loosely correlate with the day's happenings, if we can remember them in time before the active state rubs them out. In effect, things can be stored in the subconscious, over which we have no control but which can apparently affect our active state performance.

If we successfully complete something ourselves, or finish an exercise with our dogs, and then shut down, when we resume that particular exercise it will always get better. At least this is how I understand it. When I am writing, my biggest problem is always starting a chapter of a book or the opening paragraphs of an article. If I can get together a suitable start, invariably the whole thing will come together on the following day (I can only assume that Barbara Cartland sleeps a lot).

What happened with Major would seem to suggest that there is a lot more learning going on within the subconscious than we are aware of. Whenever we experienced a set-back in the training programme during the final six weeks, we stopped the training of that exercise for a few days while we considered what to do about it.

On every occasion, when we resumed the training, Major had improved from his original ability (his standard of performance before we hit problems). According to the latent learning theory as we know it, he should have got worse since we had finished on a bad note, but in fact a rest improved the performance.

For sure, by stopping we ensured that we did not compound any problems—which is something we are all guilty of when things start to go wrong: we continue to try and put them right. Perhaps the dog's reduced performance was a reaction to our change in attitude when we started to polish up his abilities (I certainly had feelings of revenge when he failed to perform). In that case, the latent learning effect was upon us, not the dog. Whatever was happening, the results were consistent: whenever we started to run into problems, we left the exercise alone for three or four days, and when we resumed, the problem disappeared and Major's performance improved.

This confused me greatly, because it suggested that the way to overcome a problem was to do nothing about it, but it happened too often to be coincidence. What also concerned me was *why* things were going wrong at all. I needed some rational explanation for why it was happening, not only before I could write about it, but for my own peace of mind. I asked various people who had all studied behavioural psychology, and although they all agreed that by stopping the exercise, rather than trying to improve it, we were ensuring that there was no increased pressure on either us or the dog, none of them could satisfactorily explain why it should improve the next time.

I eventually found the answer to both questions in two separate books.

In her book *Don't Shoot the Dog*, dolphin trainer Karen Pryor writes:

Whenever training is going on, some stress is involved, if only the stress of trying to do well. This stress may affect performance enough to mask some of the learning really taking place. At the start of the next session, before stress builds up, the performance may actually begin a step beyond where it left off, and then you have just that much more to reinforce. Shaping behaviour in this way is, of course, the opposite of training by drill and repetition.

In *Training Your Dog: The Step-by-Step Manual* by Joachim Volhard and Gail Tamases Fisher, they write:

The completion of learning is usually preceded by a learning plateau, during which the dog will give the appearance of having forgotten what he has learned. For example, during the sixth week of training, the dog, who up to now has been advancing quickly, will seem to have forgotten everything you've taught him. Be prepared for this plateau, or you will be frustrated and discouraged. Continue training, mustering all the patience you can, but don't expect too much from your dog for the next few days. Once beyond the plateau, he will be better than ever.

Both these books are American publications, and between them they explained that what Robert and I were witnessing was not a fluke, but a predictable behavioural occurrence. Whereas we did not continue training as Volhard and Fisher suggest, it would seem that there was no need to, for Major was better than ever by being left to work through it on his own. This is not to suggest that they are wrong; I am sure that, providing the handler can muster stacks of patience and not expect too much from his dog for a few days, things will work out fine. But during the period when things are going wrong there will be too much risk that the handler may fail to mask his frustration, which would have a detrimental effect on the dog. In view of what happened to us, I would advise anybody to leave the exercise alone for a few days.

Of the various opinions I sought on the subject, my APBC colleague Peter Neville earned himself a lot of Brownie points with the following explanation: 'If you were studying for an exam and reading, for example, about the hormones released by the adrenal glands during stress, you would probably find it pretty heavy-going and difficult to absorb. If you stopped and re-read the text a few days later, it would be easier to understand.' Considering Karen Pryor's explanation and my comments about latent learning in Chapter Six, I reckon that Peter was smack on; add the Volhard/Fisher learning plateau and it all makes sense.

The retrieve, searching and retrieving articles, distance control, heelwork and speak on command were all affected by this phenomenon, and when I checked our training diary, each one was within six to eight weeks from the date that it was first introduced. On reflection, I have seen this happen on many occasions in the past, but the attitude has always been: he knows what to do, make him do it. Major proved that latent learning and learning plateaux are natural parts of the dog's learning process, as are the learning curves that he demonstrated during the first few weeks.

Having established this as a fact, it further endorses my opinion that the time is right to rethink our dog training attitudes. Punishing a dog for something over which he has no control, in fact punishing him just on the point of his completing the learning process, *must be wrong*. It is an understandable reaction, considering our human attitude and our indoctrinated views on how dogs should be trained, and a trap that I nearly fell into myself.

On reflection, I am of the opinion that, regardless of the length of time a person has been training dogs, regardless of his success in the past, unless he really understands how a dog learns, he should not train another until he has found out. If he has been successful using a 'me man, you dog' approach, think what success he would have if he really knew what was happening and could do the right things at the right time, instead of the wrong things at the wrong time, which, as we found out, it is so easy to do.

It is quite probable that we would have experienced a similar problem with the 'Down—handler out of sight' exercise, but for entirely different reasons we ensured that this did not happen. In Chapter Seven I explained in some detail the importance of creating a quiet, confident attitude in the dog towards being left alone. But what we are asking the dog to do is to regulate its own behaviour in a controlled position (the down) for a long period of time.

If we are in sight and a distraction comes along, we are in a position to interrupt any ideas the dog might have about investigating the distraction by repeating the command. Out of our sight, the dog is a free agent, and if a pretty little bitch happens to trot by, it is quite likely the dog will wander over to say hello. If that pretty little bitch is in season, then you can throw all the theory out of the window—the dog will just have received a 'jackpot' reward for doing the wrong thing.

This scenario is unlikely to happen during training because, although the handler is out of sight, the instructor should be keeping a watchful eye in order to signal the handler to interrupt any movement with a further instruction. Once the initial training has been completed, the handler needs to be confident that his dog will concentrate on the job in hand. To ensure that the dog is 'bomb proof' when he has been told to stay down, we need to give him choices. What Major had already learnt was that staying down when Robert was out of sight was no big deal, in fact it was probably rewarding. What he had not learnt was what would happen if he decided to get up.

In Chapter Four I described a technique for conditioning an avoidance response in the dog, involving the use of Dog Training Discs. If you recall, they are used to suggest to the dog that the choice he has just made is not the right one and probably a complete waste of time; they also have the effect of making the dog think about what he is doing. What we intended to do, having established the fact that Major was quite confident about staying down whilst Robert was out of sight, was to teach him to concentrate on what he was doing and let him know what would happen if he chose another course of action— in other words, give him some choices to make. To do this, we needed to introduce a distraction and, because Major was very playful with other dogs, one of my own dogs was co-opted to play the role. The diagrams overleaf show how this was done.

Before we go on to investigate the learning process in more detail, I would like to record the comments of an experienced dog trainer when I explained the procedure during the time that I was researching the technique some years ago. I had by then proved how effective it was in establishing a consistent and reliable 'Down, out of sight' exercise. When I suggested that the handler should reassure the dog when it came to him, he laughed and said, 'What! Praise it for breaking the down?' At that time I really had no answer—only an intuitive feeling that we were not praising anything, we were increasing a bond. Some years on, I can explain just why this reassurance is important.

As I have already explained, what matters is the introductory conditioning technique. The dog learns that the sound is a prelude to the reward being removed. It does not constitute a physical threat, so there is no defence; it is not an extension of the owner's anger, so there is no argument; it is not used as a missile, so there is nothing to fear. In short, the dog becomes confused by the unfamiliarity of the reaction, which makes it stop its normal conditioned response and invariably seek some sort of security from the owner—as would most humans under similar circumstances.

Whenever we feel insecure, we always seek security from a higher-ranking individual. At worst, we approach an equal, but we would

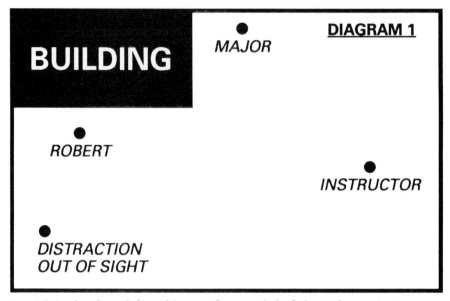

1.   *Major has been left on his own for a period of about three minutes.*

2.   *The distraction appears and Major 'chooses' to investigate, with the resulting reaction timed to coincide with his thought patterns.*

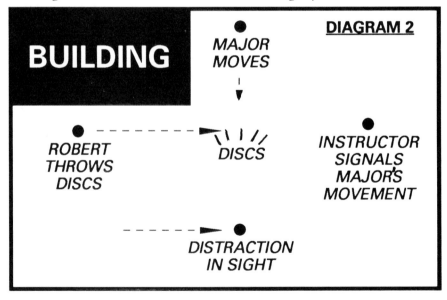

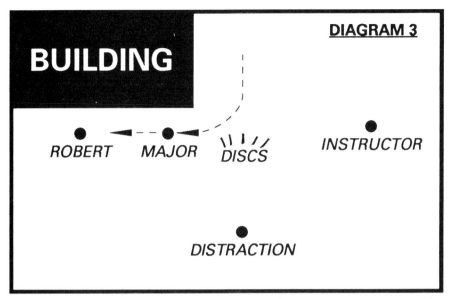

3. *Major returns to Robert for security, which Robert gives in a very calm manner, not be to construed as praise—simply, 'It's OK, don't worry.'*

4. *Robert replaces Major in the original position.*

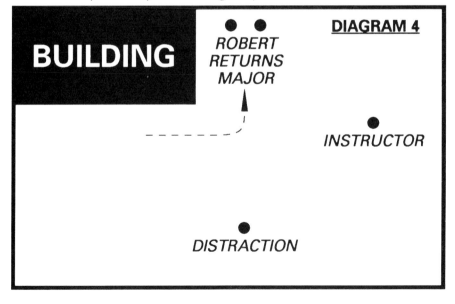

never seek security from a lower rank. The Discs create the insecurity and the handler provides the security—automatically increasing his status in the eyes of the dog.

Not only, therefore, can we teach the dog that certain actions create reactions, and stop the dog automatically reacting to a familiar and conditioned set of circumstances; we can also increase our status as far as the dog views our relationship. I can understand this trainer's reluctance to accept a non-punitive approach, and his abhorrence of reassuring a dog that has clearly just done wrong, but this brings me back to my original statement: unless we can understand how dogs learn, we should not try to train another.

We were not sure, when we set up the situation, whether Major would unthinkingly slip into his play dog mode. He had shown no signs in the past that he was likely to 'break' the down position, but because it is an exercise in which the only thing that can be varied is the location, I was of the opinion that he was learning a routine that did not require him to concentrate (as discussed in Chapter Four). As you can see from the diagrams, he did forget what he should have been doing and reacted instantly to the presence of a familiar rewarding stimulus. The Discs interrupted his thought patterns and he looked at Robert; Robert gently took him back to his original position, saying things like, 'Well, that was rather silly, but then it was your fault, old son'—reassuring noises rather than rewarding ones (my reply to the sceptical dog trainer should have been, we are reassuring a confused dog, not praising a disobedient one). He replaced him in the down position and went out of sight again. Thereafter, regardless of how many times we introduced the distraction, Major stayed where he was. What was interesting was that when we introduced the original dog, Major refused to look at it; when we introduced my two other dogs, he just showed interest in them, but did not move. Obviously an aversion to chasing after the first dog had been created, whereas other attractive stimuli made him concentrate on what he should have been doing.

It is vitally important, with regard to this particular technique, that the reader understands that the dog must be confident about being left in a controlled position with the handler out of sight, before distractions and subsequent reactions are introduced. It is not a method designed to make dogs stay down; it is designed to show the dog what will happen if it decides on another course of action. The handler's attitude would be: *I am asking you to stay in a down position whilst I pop out of sight for five or ten minutes. You have been shown how rewarding this can be, but if you choose to do anything else, it is entirely up to you—see what happens if you do.*

11

AGILITY

It was during these final six weeks that we introduced Major to the jumps. Although these exercises are not really relevant to the pet dog, it is important that you should understand the training process, because it relates just as much to anything you would want to teach your dog.

In Chapter Ten I mentioned that we had agreed to limit the requirements of Major's ability in this area because of his size in relation to his age. When fully mature, he will be expected to negotiate a six-foot high, solid vertical obstacle which has no foot-holds (it is called a scale jump and is supposed to represent a wall); a nine-foot long low jump, which not surprisingly is called a long jump and is supposed to represent a big ditch; a three-foot high obstacle called a clear jump, which is supposed to represent a gate or garden fence.

Given the right incentive, any dog which is physically fit and sufficiently agile is capable of negotiating these obstacles. I stress the fact that they must have the right incentive because, given the choice, dogs have more sense than we credit them with. The cartoon on page 126 shows us that what we expect our dogs to do can some-times appear to be quite stupid and illogical from the dog's point of view.

Stopping the dog choosing what would appear to be a sensible alternative can create problems whenever we face the dog with the obstacle. The dog says, 'Stupid! We can go round it'—the handler says, 'Bad dog! You must go over it.' Trying to explain to the dog what these jumps represent and why it is important that he should learn to negotiate them is a waste of time; so is appealing to his sense

Cartoon by Murray Ball from Punch *Magazine, 28 November, 1973. Reproduced by permission of Punch.*

of fair play by telling him that if he refuses them during the assessment, he will lose valuable marks.

As I said, dogs which are physically fit and agile can easily negotiate these obstacles. Shut a dog behind a six-foot fence and don't feed it for a few days, then watch how quickly it can scramble the fence when food is on offer. Major is a fit, agile dog, but he is also very young and very big. The wall and the ditch would represent no problem to a dog of his proportions, but landing on the other side might well do. The stresses that are placed on the still-developing bones and joints when they land off these two particular training obstacles are tremendous and, as I have already said, can cause damage which could well shorten the dog's working life.

It is heartening that people are becoming more aware of this fact, to the point that, a few years ago, dogs were banned from entering Kennel Club Working Trials until they were at least eighteen months old. This was because, even at the lowest level of Trials competition, the dog had to negotiate a six-foot scale and a nine-foot long jump (reduced for toy breeds). What was happening was that experienced competitors were training young dogs to compete as young as ten months old, and while this was not really a problem for the light-framed, extremely agile Border Collie, it could prove disastrous for the heavy-boned Rottweiler or German Shepherd Dog.

Although I personally welcomed the Kennel Club's initiative in this area, I would have preferred to see the jumps graded in height and length to suit the level of competition, with a minimum age being placed on the top level and, consequently, the biggest jumps.

As it stands at the moment, a lithe Border Collie can compete over these jumps at eighteen months, as can a heavy-boned eighteen-month-old Rottweiler. The stresses and strains on their respective bone structures are entirely different, as is their physical development.

If a dog is taught to jump properly, the risk of injury is much reduced. But considering the fact that there are few people who have the knowledge and ability to teach dogs in such a way that the landing pressures are reduced, it would be best to avoid the problem altogether. Avoiding the problem was what I intended to do with Major.

As I have said, Major is a very big dog. What I have not said is that he is very puppyish in his movement, which adds a lot to his character. Because of his size, we can easily forget how young he really is and, in particular, that he is probably undergoing more growth stress than the average dog. As this book is basically about training and not behaviour as such, suffice it to say that the hormonal surges and structural changes can affect how a dog behaves during this transitional period. My previous books *Think Dog* and *Why Does My Dog . . . ?* as well as other modern behaviour books, will explain this in more detail.

All we needed to do was teach Major that, when faced with an obstacle that he could easily go round, if Robert said, 'Over,' he meant 'go over'. At the start, height and length were not the issue, it was the principle of taking an illogical action, from the dog's point of view (go over it), rather than a logical action (go round it) that mattered.

We started with the clear jump at just 18 inches high. Robert's job was to stand beside Major in front of the jump, holding a loose leash which was to be used to stop Major going round the jump and for no other purpose. He had been instructed not to use it to increase the lift and under no circumstances, as Major landed on the other side, was there to be any checking on the collar, no matter how unintentional.

This meant that when Major jumped, Robert was going to have to move very fast. We did not use a Flexi Leash because, with too much line being reeled out, there was a danger that it might tangle with the jump and pull it over on top of the dog. My job was to stand on the other side, holding a toy for Major as the incentive to jump. He cleared it easily and was rewarded; after two more successful repetitions, we stopped.

Usually, when a dog is first introduced to the agility equipment, it is taken from one jump to the next and then to the third. Although these are all at a very manageable height, the dog is still being asked to learn three different concepts in one lesson. We wanted to make sure that Major understood and enjoyed one concept before we moved on to the next. Within three sessions over three days, he was clearing 2'6" off the leash and without a visible incentive on the other side.

Progress on the long jump was not as quick, simply because Major seemed to think that he could run across the top of it. We started it at about four feet long, and although the length was made up of individual sections, looking at it from the dog's height, it did seem like a solid ramp. We spent a couple of sessions jumping him over it with one of the elements placed on top of the other, to encourage him to gain more height, and this he did easily. However, when we went back to the original, he just ran across the top again. We realised that by raising the height of it, Major was paying more attention to what he was doing—the jump was more visible and extra effort was needed to clear it; but in effect he was learning nothing, since we needed him to make more effort on the length, not the height.

In Chapter Four I mentioned the beneficial effects of altering the routine slightly, so that the dog concentrates on what he is doing rather than reacting to familiar circumstances.

Robert had been running with Major into the jump, and I had noticed that Major kept half an eye on Robert as they approached it. It was this 'half-eye' that was stopping him from gauging the length properly, so we tried running him into it with Robert running up with him on the other side. Bingo! It worked first time. Major noticeably looked down at the jump as he approached it and cleared it by an extra three feet. It was a huge jump and an ideal moment to call a halt to the day's training. Although Robert and I had talked about how differently dogs behave when you change their familiar circumstances, he had never seen for himself how the dog takes note of everything else that is going on around him as a result of this change.

Having established that Major could easily and confidently clear a six-foot long jump—again off the leash without any visible incentive, we moved on to the scale jump.

The important aspect of teaching a dog to scale (or scramble) a vertical object is not so much how he gets up it, as how he gets down. Unfortunately, too many handlers and instructors are satisfied if the dog that they are training attacks the scale like a kangaroo, and pay little attention to the fact that it comes off the top like a free-fall parachutist, screaming GERONIMO! just before it lands with a very sharp expulsion of breath. It is not the going up that can cause the damage, it is the landing.

The Clear Jump.
Major is introduced
to a jump 18 inches
high. He is on a loose
leash, and a hand-
held toy acts as bait
on the other side.

He takes the jump
easily . . .

. . . and lands clear, with no checking on the leash by Robert.

(Below) *By his third session Major is clearing two-and-a-half feet, off the leash and with no incentive.*

The Long Jump. When Robert is on his right, Major is aware of him and fails to concentrate on the jump. Instead of jumping, he runs across the top.

By raising the jump we make Major look at it, but although he clears it he is learning nothing about its length.

When Robert stands on his left, Major noticeably pays more attention to the jump . . .

. . . and (below) clears it with three feet to spare.

The Scale jump.

I personally favour the RAF system of scaling a dog. They have the vertical surface which the dog has to negotiate, but on the other side there is a platform for the dog to land on. Alternatively, teaching the dog to negotiate what is known as an 'A' frame, which can gradually be made steeper, will train it to perform both parts of the exercise properly—the going up and the coming down.

It is very difficult to teach some breeds of dog how to do the job properly for their own protection. The Rottweiler, for example, seems to think it can fly and will try to land on all four feet at once. This is definitely better than the German Shepherd who launches himself off the top but lands on his front legs first. Neither method, however, is good for the dog. We need to teach our dogs to act like cats and slide their front feet down the other side, so that when they push off to land, they are only three feet or less from the ground.

With Major, the maximum height he would be required to scale for some months would be 4'6" (the height of the average garden wall). We actually introduced him to the scale at 4'0" because I felt

An RAF dog goes through his paces on the Scale jump.

The platform gives the dog a gentler landing than a straight drop to the ground.

The 'A' frame trains a dog to go up and down the Scale correctly.

sure that anything smaller he would have attempted to clear jump. We used the same visual incentive technique, but this time the toy was placed right at the foot of the scale just as Major reached the top. The effect was that he looked downwards instead of outwards. Not only did this teach him to come 'down' instead of 'off' the scale, it also encouraged him to get his back legs right onto the top of the jump.

   The rule about the skeletal structure of the dog, which I mentioned in discussing the 'sit' in Chapter Six, loosely applies here—if the head comes up, the bum must go down, and conversely, if the head goes down, the bum comes up. Robert's job was again to ensure that Major did not try to go round the obstacle, but also to ensure that, when he did attempt to go over it, his back legs were on top of the jump so that he did not get himself hooked on the top.

Major learns to get his back legs up on the top of the Scale.

The whole thing went like a dream. Major is an extremely agile dog for one so young and so big. It is awfully tempting for a handler, who has a dog which performs a particular exercise extremely well, to keep practising or demonstrating. Robert was warned not to do so for some months to come, which I know he will heed—he likes his dog too much to ruin him or allow him to injure himself.

I appreciate that the average pet owner would not want to teach his dog to jump over obstacles, especially obstacles the size of garden gates or fences. Naturally, I have recorded Major's progress during this part of the training because this is what I set out to do. The benefits to the pet owner really come from the lessons learned on the long jump and the attitude to the scale jump.

On the long jump, we needed to teach Major to concentrate on what he was doing—and this would apply to any other exercise.

On the scale jump, it was not what the dog was doing that was important, it was what the jump was doing to the dog.

It is unlikely that, just because a dog has been taught to jump, it will automatically become an escape artist from the garden enclosure. Dogs love to jump, and to be able to get them to do it under control only increases the relationship between you and your dog; it is just another activity from which you both benefit. I remember walking my dog past a park bench one day when I was off duty. As I went past, I tapped the top and my dog went straight over it, tail wagging like fury. An official voice said, 'You shouldn't be doing that, the benches are made for sitting on, not for dogs to jump.'

I didn't argue, I just walked off wondering why this guy had such a problem about dogs. Perhaps he had reason to; perhaps he hadn't met many trained dogs; perhaps all the dogs with which he had daily contact gave him grief.

As dog owners, we have a responsibility towards non-dog owners not to inflict our charge's anti-social behaviour upon them. If we are perfectly honest, they do have a very strong case against dogs in general, but you and I know that it is not the dogs' fault—it is the owners'.

By recording the training progress of Major, I hope that I have shown that *all* dogs are capable of achieving the same standard of expertise without weeks and weeks of drill-type training. I think that this commonly held belief—that this is the only way to train a dog— is what puts most people off making the effort. For sure, I had twelve weeks in which to train Major, but during each session we spent no more than a few minutes on each exercise, because we took the view that the dog was either learning the right thing or he wasn't. If he was not learning what we wanted, then constant negative repetition was going to teach him the wrong thing.

The agility completed Major's training and it only remained for him to be assessed on his operational abilities. I had set out to prove the theory that the time was right for a change in dog training attitudes and I was fortunate in having a very capable dog and a very receptive handler. Regardless of how the assessment went, what I think we did prove was that, providing the dog understands what to do and the incentive to do it is there, it can learn surprisingly quickly. The only thing that can spoil that learning process is we humans and our misplaced, indoctrinated attitude towards the dog.

12

ASSESSMENT DAY

This is probably the easiest chapter to write, because it is simply a record of what happened on the day of Robert and Major's test. The whole idea of the exercise had been to train Major to a standard equivalent to the Home Office standard for Police Dogs, but at the same time to look at how these training techniques could transfer just as easily to the pet dog. I was very fortunate that I had been given the usual twelve weeks in which to complete the training but, to my own satisfaction, I proved that it can be done in much less time, simply by avoiding the negative side of traditional dog training.

Throughout his training, Major had not once been told that he was wrong when he did not perform an exercise properly. The word 'no' was not part of the training vocabulary which he learned—unlike most dogs who must eventually think that their name is No! Special emphasis was placed on Major learning the meaning of the words of command and not just the routine exercise in which these words simply become the cue to the next movement. In effect, we taught him rather than conditioned him.

For the pet dog owner's benefit, it should be noted that we did not train Major to this standard by hitting him with rolled-up newspapers, or shaking him by the scruff of the neck (which is supposed to represent the mother's disciplinary procedure, but if you ask any breeder, they will tell you that this very rarely happens); we did not smack him, nag him, yank on a choke chain, shut him in another room or refuse to speak to him for the rest of the day. If we punished him at all, it was by withholding any reward.

The end result, as you will see, was that they both completed the assessment with flying colours. I say both, because that is what dog

Assessment day—the moment of truth.

training is all about—forming a working or social relationship between man and dog. A social relationship means that both the dog and the owner behave in a socially acceptable manner together.

With such a strong anti-dog lobby in this country today, it is no longer acceptable to take the view 'love me, love my dog'. All dog owners have a responsibility to see that their dog's bad behaviour is not inflicted upon other people, and one of the ways to do this is to ensure that they are trained properly. What we had done with Major, you can do with your dog, and the degree of polish you achieve in the way your dog performs the exercises depends only on how much you practise. Teaching them to do them in the first place, as you will have seen, is relatively easy, and once they understand, they learn. Of course, if you don't occasionally remind them, they will forget, and therefore a certain amount of repetition is needed; but contrary to what the Home Office Manual and an awful lot of dog training books state, they don't *learn* through constant repetition.

Using the score sheets on the following pages, it would be an interesting experiment to conduct an informal test of your own on the exercises that you have taught your dog.

For comparison, you can see the marks awarded by the two judges for Major's performance.

I was naturally very pleased with the performance of both Robert and Major. I could tell as soon as the first exercise started that Robert was nervous: not—he told me later—because he doubted Major's ability to perform well, but because he knew that I wanted him to turn in the performance of his life, to give written proof of my theories. This was not something we had talked about and, with hindsight, I should have realised that Robert knew how important it was to me for him to do well, and relieved him of this pressure. Not doing so resulted in Major sensing Robert's change of attitude and being slightly 'bouncy' during the heelwork exercise; the fact that he developed an itch, which just had to be scratched, during the 'Stand when marching' was nobody's fault other than whatever bit him. His over-eagerness during the Chase exercise in the Man Work section caused him to go before he had been told, and to use the usual dog owner's excuse, 'Well! He's never done that before', did not impress either judge and resulted in a loss of ten points from each of them.

OBEDIENCE		POSSIBLE	EXAMINERS	
			FIRST	SECOND
Heel Free	Walking to heel	20	18	16
	Leaving dog in sit	5	5	5
	Leaving dog in down	5	5	4
	Leaving dog in stand	5	5	5
	Leaving dog in sit when marching	5	5	5
	Leaving dog in down when marching	5	5	5
	Leaving dog in stand when marching (calling dog to heel on direction)	5	4	–
	Retrieve	10	10	9
	Distant control finishing with recall	10	10	10
	Speak on command	10	8	8
	Down out of sight (5 minutes)	20	20	20
	TOTAL	100	95	87

AGILITY

		POSSIBLE	FIRST	SECOND
	Hurdles (height 3ft)	10	10	10
	Long jump (length 6ft)	20	18	15
	Scale (height 4ft 6ins) (Mark on control as well as agility)	20	20	20
	TOTAL	50	48	45

| | EXAMINERS | | |
SEARCHING FOR PROPERTY	POSSIBLE	FIRST	SECOND
4 Articles in square 12yds × 12yds 5 minutes allowed 20 marks for each article			
Handler not allowed in square	80	80	80
Retrieving buried article	20	20	20
TOTAL	100	100	100

MAN WORK

	POSSIBLE	FIRST	SECOND
Searching for person (mark for quartering and speaking)	50	50	50
Crowd control	20	20	20
Test of courage (stick chase)	50	50	50
Chase (dogs will be required to be off the lead before 'chase' in the down position)	50	40	40
Marks will be given for control on 'leave'			
TOTAL	170	160	160

TRACKING

	POSSIBLE	FIRST	SECOND
Track to include at least 3 turns	80	80	80
TOTAL	80	80	80
OVERALL MARKS	500	483	472

In no way did these minor faults detract from his obvious abilities, and since one judge awarded him 94 per cent and the other awarded him 97 per cent (giving a joint overall score of 95.5 per cent), they were obviously of the same opinion.

These methods can be applied to your own dog. How much or how little you want it to learn is entirely your decision, but I hope that the information contained within these pages will help you teach your dog in a way that it will easily understand, and without having to resort to punishment. I am convinced that if we can really think about what we are trying to teach, and at the same time think about what the dog might really be learning, we shall start to see things in a different light. If we can do this, perhaps we can start to change the anti-dog brigade's attitude towards dogs within our modern society.

After more than 10,000 years of a successful relationship between man and dog, there has never been so much pressure put on it as there is today. It is time for changes in attitude to be made, and as dog owners, the responsibility is on us to make these changes, whether we like it or not. It is time to 'get modern' and realise that how we used to train dogs does not correlate with our new lifestyle.

I am convinced that this is also the reason why there is now a need for people who do the kind of work that I do. Doggy people who have been involved in the world of dogs for forty, even fifty years, will still frown on the need for behaviour counsellors; that is because they would never allow a problem to arise in the first place—or so they think. The modern way of life, the new diets that are available, the increased knowledge that allows the veterinary profession to prolong a dog's useful life, have all created problems that we never had to face before. For example, how can 'training' a dog which has just lost its hearing through old age stop it howling when it has been left at home while the owner goes shopping? It's a direct result of improved health care and a natural anxiety within the dog that it has lost one of its vital senses. How can 'training' a dog stop it from reacting to certain chemicals in the food or the water, which never used to be there before we started to treat our pets as 'special people' and a viable commercial target? This is not yet proven but under investigation. How can 'training' a dog overcome the effects of reduced exercise and the corresponding lack of mental stimulus that it used to receive before, when we walked the dog from A to B instead of driving it there? It is a direct result of our increasingly affluent society.

These and many other factors should be taken into account before we decide whether we have taken on a 'bad dog' or not. In most cases, what is missing is a lack of proper understanding and the wrong approach to training. I hope that what I have written will redress this imbalance slightly; if not, I would strongly advise you to ask your veterinary surgeon to refer you on to someone who will be able to help you further. The final chapter of this book will give you some guidance on where to go for this help.

13

HELP WITH BEHAVIOUR PROBLEMS

Since specialising in problem dogs, much of what I have seen and learnt has helped me to improve my training techniques, not just with my own dogs, but also, in one instance, with a particularly awkward young Irish pony that we own. Not that I am claiming to have any special knowledge about training horses, but it shows that the positive approach to training applies, as I stated earlier, to all animals that are capable of learning. Although, as a result of specialising, I have learnt more about my basic training skills, it does not alter my original observations: there are still dogs who are incapable of learning because something is blocking their ability to do so.

As a member of the Association of Pet Behaviour Counsellors, working as I do strictly on veterinary referral, I do not need to possess any particular scientific knowledge to do my job. I can assume before I see the dog that the vet has ruled out any medical involvement, and if I suspect one, I can refer the dog back to have it checked out. Sometimes this does happen, simply because I get the opportunity to see each dog for a session that can last up to two hours, whereas the vet generally does not have that luxury during surgery hours. As one vet recently stated, the benefit he gets from having a behavioural referral service is that we have the time to find out what's gone wrong and then point him in the right direction if there is also some medical attention needed. This might sound as though we are expected to diagnose physical ailments; it is not intended in that way, although some of the APBC member practices also have veterinary qualifications and are qualified to do so. A recent case that I dealt with should explain how a lay person involved with behaviour therapy can work hand in hand with the referring veterinary surgeon.

The details in the appointment book said: 'Mrs Jones (name changed) with "depressed" Rottweiler.' At the appointed time, Mrs Jones arrived, dragging behind her a very sad-looking Rottie. She sat down and immediately embarked upon a history of her obviously very unhappy domestic circumstances. All the children had left home as a result of ongoing arguments; her husband was an alcoholic who often became violent; even her dog (the depressed Rottweiler) would have nothing to do with her—in fact the last time her husband had attacked and tried to strangle her, the Rottie had joined in whilst she was flat on her back on the floor trying to fight off her husband.

As I listened to what she was telling me, I was doing two other things: I was watching the dog, who had chosen to lie down as far away from us as possible and was facing the wall rather than us; and I was reading the notes that the referring vet had sent to me. He suspected a hypothyroid problem (which would result in a very lethargic attitude in the dog). However, in view of the massive domestic problems that Mrs Jones had tried to explain to him, he could understand that there was much more involved than just testing and treating the dog. In short, he was not sure that by just treating the thyroid problem he would be treating the whole problem; he was not even sure whether the symptom was medical or behavioural and, with a waiting room full of patients, he did not have the time to find out.

In my opinion, although there was an awful lot of behavioural counselling involved, in particular because Mrs Jones was relying on her dog to stay faithful to her when every other member of the household had let her down, the dog was not behaving in the way I would have expected under the circumstances. I advised a programme which was designed to make the dog more reliant upon Mrs Jones, rather than the other way round, and asked the vet to run up some thyroid tests. It transpired that the vet was spot on with his initial diagnosis: there was a medical problem but one that needed some behavioural advice to coincide with the treatment if it was to prove effective.

One of the comments I received when I was discussing this with a colleague was that Mrs Jones would be better off owning a cat. Under the circumstances that was probably true: any dog is likely to exhibit behaviour problems living in such a stressful environment—as would a cat, but cats are just as likely to find themselves another home, whereas dogs don't do that. But for me to have told this lady, who was already bordering on a nervous breakdown, that she should re-home her dog would have pushed her right over the edge. As she saw it, her whole family had turned against her and now the dog was following suit. By treating the thyroid problem and getting her to understand that dogs cannot cope with ongoing stressful situations without changes in their behaviour patterns, I was able to make her feel more sorry for the dog than she was for herself.

For the sake of the dog, I would have preferred to recommend that he be re-homed, but sometimes we have to accept the fact, unfortunate though it is, that one of the functions of the modern dog is to act as a sponge to soak up the stresses of today's environment. Her dog had a role to play in preserving her sanity, even if it was just by making her realise that it needed her help. Trying to 'train' her dog would have been a waste of time. Had it been 'trainable', this would not have overcome the problem; it needed a combination of veterinary care, canine behaviour counselling and a touch of human psychology.

This was a sad case in which the prognosis for a total cure was not good; all I could report back to the vet was that there would be an improvement. Admittedly, not all my work-load is as involved as this, but most cases require me to delve into the domestic circumstances in which the dog lives, and I quite often have to drag some skeletons out of people's cupboards. Behaviour therapy for dogs involves a variety of skills, both academic and practical. They say that a little knowledge is dangerous and I would agree, unless one recognises one's own limitations. In the case of the depressed Rottweiler, I only needed to be able to recognise that the dog was not behaving as I would expect a well dog to behave.

I did not need to be able to recognise possible thyroid dysfunction because, in the words of the TV advertisement, I know a man who can; now that there is an Association of Pet Behaviour Counsellors, I know lots of men and women who can.

The APBC was formed in 1989 following a meeting of like-minded individuals who were all engaged on a full-time basis with behaviour problems in either dogs or cats. I am proud to say that I was one of the founding fathers of this organisation which, since its inaugural meeting, has gone from strength to strength in a relatively short time. As I write, there are approximately 40 clinics scattered around England, Ireland and Scotland, most of them held at veterinary establishments, including three of the United Kingdom's veterinary schools, with some also at animal charity centres.

The strength of the APBC lies in the variety of backgrounds from which its members come—veterinary medicine, clinical psychology, biology, zoology, ethology—as well as including some of the leading experts in the field of training, who between them have many years' experience in police dog, guide dog and pet dog training. The Association also enjoys the membership of some of the foremost behaviourists from overseas and is backed up by a team of veterinary advisers. With this enormous pool of knowledge available to every member for the cost of a phone call, we can offer the veterinary profession a referral service of the highest possible standard. As I said earlier, if one of us doesn't know, we all know someone who does, and between member practices this knowledge is freely available.

The formation of the Association has proved especially useful from a research point of view—for example we are able to collect nation-wide data on specific problems, and at the time of writing we are studying dog-to-dog aggression. We hope to be able to look at a specific problem every year: with the input from a variety of sources all over the country, we should gain a much better understanding of the problem and, what is more important, how to cure it.

The results of our research will be published in our annual report and, of course, through the popular dog press. For the past three years we have held an APBC symposium at Warwick University and already this has become a major event in the calendars of interested people—the 1992 symposium attracted a capacity audience of 500 people over two days.

We are also organising 'in house' educational courses for member practices and their associates, where we can learn from each other's specialist skills. One of my associates, Jeri Vogwill, as well as having a first degree in psychology, also has a master's degree in counsellor education. She is conducting a residential course for the APBC to help us improve our individual counselling skills, and future courses of this nature are under discussion.

All in all, it is a very exciting time for anyone involved in the field of problem behaviour in companion animals, especially dogs, but as I said in Chapter Two, we should not lose sight of the fact that dogs still need to be taught some basic obedience. This means that a better understanding of the dog's behaviour should go hand in hand with improved training techniques, not one instead of the other.

For one reason or another some dogs exhibit particularly resistant problem behaviour patterns, and if you are unfortunate enough to own a dog like this you are going to need some professional help. In the first instance, you should consult your veterinary surgeon with a view to being referred to an APBC practice in your area—details of my practice and the headquarters of my colleagues will be found in the Appendix.

Many of the pet insurance companies cover partly or in full the fees of APBC members and most cases are seen for a session which lasts about two hours, with both the client and the referring vet receiving follow-up reports. Except for severe cases of aggression, one consultation is usually all that is required, since contact is maintained by phone as the rehabilitation programme progresses.

I hope that what I have described in this book will be sufficient to help you overcome any problem that you might be experiencing, without having to consult someone else. Often, it is just one snippet of information or one alternative approach that helps people to reach the 'AH-HA' level—'AH-HA! That's where I'm going wrong.' If there is a snippet in this book which helps you, then even if you reject everything else that I have said, the recording of my experiment with Major has been worthwhile.

With an average assessment pass mark of 95.5 per cent, the experiment was clearly worthwhile from Robert's point of view. Considering that at no time during the course was Major reprimanded, physically manhandled or negatively corrected for getting it wrong, I feel sure that if the dog himself were able to read and I showed him the manual of how he would normally have been trained, he, too, would consider the experiment to have been a success.

To a lot of people, training a dog without resorting to punishment for unwanted behaviour is a concept that is hard to grasp. Robert proved with Major that this was possible, so it can be done. At the end of the assessment we had a celebratory drink, during which the examiners found out for the first time that we had rejected the traditional 'tell 'em–make 'em–praise 'em' approach and that Major had been trained by giving him choices and leaving it to him to learn which one was the best to take. Robert's comment during the discussion summed up the whole concept:

'I wish that I had been taught like that when I was at school.'

EPILOGUE

Some months later, I am pleased to report that Robert and Major are successfully operational on Hampstead Heath, and already Major has proved himself, on quite a few occasions, to be an effective member of the dog section.

I see all the section's dogs on a regular basis during their refresher training duties and find that Major has matured into a happy, confident working dog. His performance is as good as some and better than most, but what does stand out when he is training alongside the other dogs is his attitude to what he is doing. He clearly enjoys everything he does and I am convinced that this is because there is not one doubt in his mind that he might be wrong, or that he might be told off if he gets it wrong. He no longer needs the reinforcement of food or a toy, although occasionally Robert does surprise him.

Standing back and watching them work gives me an enormous feeling of pride and satisfaction and has taught me yet another lesson which I did not expect to learn when we started the experiment. Dogs that are trained using these techniques eventually end up reinforcing their own behaviour, simply through the sheer joy of performing the exercise and the obvious pleasure that they give to their working partner.

ASSOCIATION OF PET
BEHAVIOUR COUNSELLORS

APPENDIX:
THE ASSOCIATION OF PET BEHAVIOUR COUNSELLORS

Richard Allport, BVetMed, VetMF Hom, MRCVS, 11 Southgate Road, Potters Bar, Herts. EN6 5DR.

David Appleby and Associates, Dog and Cat Help, Upper Street, Defford, Worcs. WR8 9AB.

Bruce Englefield, Beaples Hill Farm, Knowstone, South Motton, Devon EX36 4RZ.

Kym Lawrence, Bickleigh Behaviour Centre, 132 Soundwell Road, Soundwell, Bristol BS16 4RT.

Emma Magnus, MSc, The Chequers Inn, Raydon, Ipswich, Suffolk IP7 5LW.

Marie Miller, 01203 366090 (puppy classes).

Gwen Bailey, BSc(Hons), The Blue Cross, Shilton Road, Burford, Oxon. OX18 4PF.

Caroline Bower, BVM&S, MRCVS, Veterinary Health Centre, 16 Branson Court, Upper Chaddlewood, Plympton, Plymouth, Devon PL7 3WU.

Donna Brander and Associates, Kirkhouse Farm, Dolphinton, Peebleshire EH46 7AF.

Dr Natalie Warren, University of Edinburgh, IERM, School of Agriculture Building, Wl Mains Road, Edinburgh EH9 3JG.

Alison Boyle, 32 Millfield Drive, Erskine, Renfrewshire PA8 6JA.

John Fisher and Associates, Greengarth, Maddox Lane, Bookham, Surrey KT23 3HT.

Sally Chandler, Cherry Tree Cottage, Coughton Hall Avenue, Send, Woking, Surrey GU23 7DE.

Julie Morgan, 1 Park View, Sutton Green Road, Sutton Green, Surrey.

Jacqui Pritchard, 23 Arkwright Drive, Binfield, Bracknell, Berks. RG12 1FX.

Peter Neville, DHc, BSc(Hons), and Associates, 53 March Court, Warwick Drive, London SW15 6LE.

Jenny Adams, Leaders Dog Training and Pet Behaviour, 9 Cramlington Terrace, West Allotment, Newcastle-on-Tyne NE27 0DX.

Charlie Clarricoates, Scampers School for Dogs, Crow Hall, Northfield Road, Soham, Nr. Ely, Cambs. CB4 5LD.

Sarah Whitehead, BA(Hons), c/o 4 Quarry Cottages, Chicksgrove, Salisbury, Wilts. SP3 6LZ.

Robin Walker, BVetMed, MRCVS, The Gables Veterinary Group, 78 Bromyard Road, Worcester WR2 5DA.

Margaret Goddard, BVSc, MRCVS, Endell Veterinary Group, 49 Endless Street, Salisbury, Wilts. SP1 3UH.

Claire Guest, BSc(Hons), Hearing Dogs for the Deaf, London Road, Lewknor, Oxon. OX9 5RY.

Sarah Heath, BVSc, MRCVS, Croft Veterinary Centre, Banbury Road, Brackley, Northants. NN13 6BH.

Ann McBride, BSc, PhD, FRSA, and Associate, 1A Courtland Gardens, Bassett, Southampton SO2 3PP.

Colette Kase, 142 Bramley Close, Higham Hill, London E17.

Valerie O'Farrell, PhD, 7 Braid Road, Edinburgh EH10 6AE.

Jeri Omlo, BS MEd, 8 Stannary Road, Stenalees, St Austell, Cornwall PL26 8SP.

Hazel Palmer, 48 Ridley Road, Forest Gate, London E7 0LT.

Katie Patmore, CQSW, 39 Banner Cross Road, Sheffield S11 9HQ.

Erica Peachey, BSc(Hons), 37 Lang Lane, West Kirby, Wirral, Merseyside L48 5HQ.

Christopher Ross, BVM&S, MRCVS, Braid Veterinary Hospital, 171 Mayfield Road, Edinburgh EH9 3AZ.

Alison Rowbotham, 58 Arch Street, Rugeley, Staffs. WS15 1DL.

Julie Sellors, Parklands, Station Road, Topcliffe, Thirsk, N. Yorks. YO7 3SE.

Overseas Member Practices

Dr Roger Abrantes, DF, Etologisk Institut, Lille Fredrikslund, DK-4200, Singelse, Denmark.

Prof. R. K. Anderson, DVM, 511 Eleventh Avenue South, Minneapolis, MN 55415-1436, USA.

Prof. Nicholas Dodman, DVA, BVM&S, MRCVS, School of Veterinary Medicine, Tufts University, North Grafton, MA 01536, USA.

Mrs Ruth Foster (address as for Prof. R. K. Anderson).

Dany Grosemans, Weyerstraat 33, 3545 Halen-Zelem, Belgium.

Dr Paul McGreevy, BVSc, MRCVS, PhD, Department of Animal Science, University of Sydney, Sydney, NSW 2006, Australia.

Mrs Terry Ryan, NW 2025 Friel Street, Pullman, Washington 99163, USA.

George Quinlan, PO Box 7781, Bend, OR 97708-7781, USA.

Dr Dennis Turner, Pet Counsulting, IET, Vorderi Siten 30, CH-8816, Hirzel, Switzerland.

For more information about the APBC you should contact the Hon Secretary, Association of Pet Behaviour Counsellors, 257 Royal College Street, London NW1 9LU.

INDEX

Page numbers in bold type refer to main entries in text

162   DOGWISE

training – *cont'd.*
   target, 110
   whistle, **50**
trophy, 39

urinate, 20

values:
   canine, 10

   human, 10
veterinary surgeons, 8, 12, 38,
   81, 101, 103, 147, 149, 151,
   153
visitors, 8

whistle, 40, **50**
withers, 33, 49
wolf, 7, 35, 39